The Hapha

A story of two pioneers with a dream - and their daughter Penelope who with their son-in-law Philip further developed their visionary planting at Orchards, Rowfant, Sussex; formerly the home and garden of Arthur George Lee Hellyer and Grace Charlotte Hellyer

Penelope S Hellyer.

Penelope S Hellyer

Published in 2012 by FeedARead.com Publishing
Arts Council funded

A CIP catalogue record for this title is available from
the British Library.

Acknowledgements

In chronological order I must thank Arthur and Gay for their passion and resilience during the first years of their marriage; when against Arthur's better judgement they purchased the land on which they built a house and ran a market garden through very difficult times. Without this early start the garden could never have evolved.

I thank my daughter Sorcha who has constantly believed in me and in my capabilities. I am grateful for her encouragement through my negative years and her continuing positivity in all that I undertake.

To Philip, my husband; whose love and endless support has enhanced my life and shows no lessening. During our time together, no matter which venture I have embarked upon, he has always been my most stalwart supporter. He doesn't waver in his devotion to me and for this I am eternally appreciative.

Thanks must also go to the late Rosemary Verey who became my mentor and friend. She selflessly gave time and nurture to me after Gay's death.

Profound thanks to all of the volunteers who helped in any way whilst we worked in the garden. Their assistance was invaluable and our task would have been so much more arduous without them. Especially to Annie Bridges - who made the best carrot cake I have ever tasted and gave copious amounts of time, energy and home baking to our various garden open days for charity.

In particular I thank Chris Coomber; a work colleague who became one of our most valuable volunteers and a long-term friend.

To Vikki Heasman; willing, flexible, amusing and hardworking. She was my 'companion' gardener for the last few years at Orchards and made my work easier during my period of ill health. She too remains a good friend.

Stuart Cooksey; whose friendship was often tested by the conditions he worked in. Frequently he would leave the garden soaked to the skin in his attempt to complete the grass cutting.

Peter Freeland, one of Gay's former pupils whose help with a contact list of many of her other past students enabled me to get a fuller picture of Gay the teacher. He also prepared several pages of his own reminiscences for me to draw on.

Lastly, thanks go to Sue Johnson, my course tutor at Writers' News Home Study. She helped me see beyond the fog, until I found the maze; through which she guided me, instilling confidence and giving me the inspiration to link together pieces I had written since 2002; enlarging the original manuscript, and through an extension to my course, to complete this book.

Contents

Prologue

Arthur George Lee Hellyer and his wife Grace Charlotte née Bolt (known as Gay), were the inspiration behind the garden, the house at Orchards and this book. This book is not a biography of my parents. It is the story of my childhood, my early womanhood and my final sixteen years at Orchards. There is a brief account of them and their time at Orchards because without a couple of chapters about them, there would be no story for me to tell.

I wasn't told their reasons for buying this plot of land and various pieces written about Arthur over the years are contradictory. Neither did I know their long term intentions. What I do know, from the black and white photographs that are in my possession, is what it looked like when they arrived. It has to be remembered in this story that Arthur and Gay had been working together at Orchards for fifteen years before I come on the scene. I have childhood memories and a few stories to tell but my work in the garden begins in 1968 and the hard work ten years later.

When I began the text for this book during convalescence from major surgery in the winter of 2002

I had written the following: 'This book can have no ending whilst I remain at Orchards, the sights, the sounds, the perfumes, flowery trails of memory. I could not remove the straggly unnamed *Hebe* - an old black and white picture shows me pruning it aged nine or ten. In another picture for insertion in one of his books, Arthur stands secateurs to the ready. Even from within the house the garden was with you. Every window sets a scene; the nets on the bathroom window drawn during hand washing or bathroom cleaning to catch a glimpse.

And yet, now I no longer live at Orchards, the garden continues to evolve. It has become a sanctuary for another very fortunate family. The Anslies' the current owners keep in contact with me and Hamish refers to me as the 'oracle'.

How my life has changed since I started this text in 2002 - a chance comment from a gardening acquaintance gave me the idea for the title of this book; when once again she criticised my way of doing things. By now experience had taught me that a lot of hard work and many of the gardening rules had to be broken to achieve what I wanted to accomplish. From 1989 I gardened more than seven acres - with help from my husband Philip whose working day started at 6am and from 1994 with occasional help from volunteers. With the exception of the last three years I was working by myself.

Part One

Chapter One

Photograph by Navana Vandyk

Arthur George Lee Hellyer
MBE VHM FLS AHRHS

Arthur George Lee Hellyer was born on 16 December 1902 at 15 Hartington Park, Redland, Clifton, Bristol; the second child of Arthur Lee Hellyer and his wife Maggie née Parlett. His sister, Margaret Irene Lee Hellyer was born in 1899.

He was educated at Manor House School in Clapham Common and then at Dulwich College, Dulwich Common, London. He left Dulwich College in April 1918 whilst still in the Upper Fourth at the age of fifteen. He had contracted tuberculosis. The family doctor recommended a life in the open air. His first gardening experience in 1915/1916 was digging up the lawn in the family garden to grow vegetables. He remembers finding a '*new world of delight*' in the two books he was reading during this period - Cousins' *Chemistry of the Garden* and H H Thomas' *Complete Gardener*.

By August 1918 he was working in Guernsey on a tomato farm, his sister and parents were with him. His sister Rene describes in a letter to her Grandmamma, the house they are to rent. *'It stands in a row of about six and is surrounded by fields. In front is a large enclosed common belonging to the Fort, where the militia camp out. This is really the only objection to the house, but the soldiers here seem well behaved.'* Rene continues, *'The situation is lovely; the whole of the north of the Island lies spread out before you like a map. Daddy thinks of getting Arthur a small motorbicycle to take him to Mr Harwood's and help him up the terrible hills here.'* I have a photograph of the house in my possession - it is a very large grand square house.

From Guernsey he went to Jersey where he worked on the States of Jersey Experimental Farm and then as a labourer for Mr Bree, a farmer, in La Sente, La Rocque. He must have felt very comfortable with his surroundings as his mother Maggie was a Jersey girl. Her father, George William Parlett, married Eliza Malzard, from a very old Jersey family. As a boy Arthur spent most of his school holidays in Jersey staying in rented accommodation in Sameres and then in La Rocque. Parlett and Malzard members of the family were still living there. In the 1920s he returned for holidays staying with his aunt Lily Parlett. It was also where his father - the State Auditor for Jersey - paid four visits yearly before renting a house at La Rocque. In 1921 his father died at the age of forty-eight and the family moved back to Bristol taking Maggie's aging father with them.

In Bristol, Arthur worked first as a nursery boy for Isaac House & Sons earning twelve shillings and sixpence per week; this rose to fifteen shillings and five years later he was earning three pounds per week, as he had as a farm labourer in Jersey. Within a few years Arthur the nursery boy (carrying the propagator's tools), became propagator, moving on to become their

17

chief salesman. This job involved setting up exhibits at the major flower shows. I believe it was here that he would have begun to make some of the contacts that would influence his later career.

Isaac House & Sons began as a market garden at Coombe Nursery, Canford Lane, Westbury-on-Trym. In the 1891 census Isaac is shown as a market gardener and florist. He was born about 1833; when Arthur joined his business Isaac was in his eighties. Isaac's son James C House was now specialising in herbaceous perennials and alpine plants. Arthur and he developed the Causican scabious, introducing several new cultivars one of which, *Scabiosa caucasica* 'Clive Greaves', is still widely available. House & Sons exhibited at the first Southport show in 1924. Arthur fell out with Isaac House after setting up an exhibit without the help of House at a large show and winning a gold medal. He asked House for a rise, House refused so Arthur left.

He took a job at Wilson & Agar's nursery in Twyford, Berkshire for one winter before returning to Bristol where he worked as Nursery Manager for Luke Rogers & Sons. Luke Rogers & Sons is listed in trade directories, throughout the 1920s and 1930s as a

'Florists and Garden Craftsmen', to a Seed and Bulb Merchants with a Florists Shop in Whiteladies Road, Bristol in the late 1960s.

It was at this time that Arthur started to write. The story varies but the one that Arthur told me was of visiting a nursery relative in Dublin. During this visit he met with a young lady, who, whilst working as a jobbing gardener, also wrote articles about gardening and plants for local newspapers. Arthur realised that he actually knew more about gardening than she did. On his return home, he wrote an article and sent it to Gardening Illustrated; it was rejected. He sent a second article to A J Macself then editor of Amateur Gardening which was accepted. It was not so much an article more a 'piece'. On the 'Flower Garden Notes' page of the 1 October 1927 edition of Amateur Gardening Magazine this brief snippet about *Perovskia atriplicifolia* read: '*The subject of this note is a useful and not too well known shrub, somewhat reminiscent of a tall and much stiffer catmint. The flowers, produced in August and September, are of a similar form and colour to this well-known and useful plant, though rather smaller and of a yet more distinctly powder blue shade. They are borne in fine sprays on good, stiff*

19

stems. The grey-green foliage is small and neat, and has an agreeable scent. The flowers last quite well when cut, and are admirable for arranging with other subjects. It does well in any good garden soil, relishing a warm, sunny position, and attains a height of some five feet when quite at home.' - A. H.-. One hundred and seventeen words in total. In those days initials were the only acknowledgement given to the author. On this same page are two snippets of greater length attributed to A.T.J. who I surmise to be the late, great A T Johnson. Arthur was overwhelmed by his first publication. This small beginning was to lead to a long and illustrious career. It is obvious from the research that I have done and from the letters that I have in my archive that Macself liked Hellyer; continuing to employ Arthur as a freelance contributor over the next couple of years.

In a magazine profile in 1987 Arthur said that *'accident had largely determined his life.'* Directed by illness to an outside job he seems to have fallen easily into the profession he was to follow for more than sixty years. He met, by good fortune, T W Sanders at that time editor of Amateur Gardening, whilst holidaying on the island of Jersey in 1925. Sanders was there with his invalid daughter. Arthur asked what prospects there were for a young man in horticultural journalism. Sanders replied, '*None whatsoever. I have one assistant editor who has been with me for thirty years and when he dies I will need one replacement.*' Sanders had been appointed assistant editor to the first editor of Amateur Gardening Magazine, James Shirley Hibberd in 1884. When Sanders was offered the editorship a couple of years later, he initially agreed to a one year trial unsure of his capability in the role - he held the position for approximately forty years until his death in 1926. Sanders assistant, A J Macself then became editor of Amateur Gardening.

Arthur had spoken briefly to Macself at the Royal Agricultural Society Show in Reading in 1925 where Macself was judging the horticultural section. After Sanders death Arthur sent an article with a covering letter to Macself - who remembered the young Hellyer. In 1928 Macself asked Arthur to be his assistant editor on Commercial Horticulture, a new trade paper. Arthur accepted, but due to lack of advertising the paper folded after six months. In a letter dated 6 January 1929 Macself wrote to Arthur asking, '*Do you happen to know a competent young man who has a bent for*

21

horticultural journalism & who would be interested in an opportunity to work under me as an assistant editor.' Arthur swiftly replied '*Me*'.

A J Macself

By February 1929 Arthur was second assistant editor at Amateur Gardening, with Henry A Smith being the first. Arthur worked with Smith, superseding Smith as editor in 1946. Smith retired a few years later. Arthur was also editor of Gardening Illustrated from 1947-1956.

This was the beginning of his life's work. *'The Amateur Gardening Pocket Guide'* first printed in 1941, was conceived by Arthur and for him it was his greatest accolade. One hundred and twenty thousand words of gardening advice printed on bible-thin paper in small type. The original was no bigger than a pocket diary.

Arthur was to write or revise more than thirty books during his long career. His grounding as a nurseryman and his diligence given to the revision and modernisation of T W Sanders '*Encyclopaedia of Gardening*' taught him his trade well. The original book was first serialised in Amateur Gardening Magazine at the end of the 19th century. The revision of this book Arthur claimed was, *'far beyond my capabilities at the time'*. Arthur's book '*Simple Rose Growing*, published in 1930, appears to be his first publication. It took him a couple of years to revise and update Sanders '*Alphabet of Gardening*', in its foreword Arthur remarks that, '*For half a century his books [T W Sanders] have held a unique place in the gardening world, and they have served to instruct hundreds of thousands of amateurs - and not a few professionals, too, be it added - in the horticultural art.'* Arthur's books are now lauded in the same way by other professional garden writers and horticulturalists.

He wrote articles for several prestigious magazines, gave talks and sat on many garden-question panels. During his career as editor of Amateur Gardening, the magazine's circulation rose substantially. In many ways Orchards was his 'outdoor laboratory' -

photographs for various articles and features in Amateur Gardening magazine and several of his books were illustrated with pictures taken at Orchards.

Throughout his long career in horticulture Arthur's involvement with the Royal Horticultural Society (RHS) spanned most of his working life. He was appointed to the RHS Floral 'A' committee in 1947. He judged at the RHS shows, at Chelsea, other major horticultural shows and at the trial grounds at Wisley. He served the RHS until a few weeks before his death.

Arthur's reply to a letter from Brigadier Lycett in 1953 informing him he was being offered an RHS Associate of Honour and enquiring if he would accept it shows the modesty and humour which characterised Arthur. Arthur's letter begins, *'No man was ever more surprised than I was when I opened your letter this morning! I had no idea I had done anything to justify any sort of recognition by the Royal Horticultural Society and I am certainly most grateful to the president and the council for doing me this wholly unexpected honour'.* A further honour of Vice President of the RHS was bestowed upon him in 1981.

In 1959 he became the first gardening correspondent for the Saturday Financial Times joined in 1970 by

Robin Lane Fox. Robin still acknowledges Arthur's important contribution to the horticulture world, in several articles published since Arthur's death. In an article on 2 April 2005 he describes Arthur's book *'Your Garden Week by Week'* as a masterpiece and the 1993 reprint outclasses any other gardening guide he knows. In 1982 Arthur was presented with The Dean Hole Medal for his contribution to the classification of rose species. This medal is awarded by the Royal National Rose Society. He also had a great involvement with various charities in one way or another.

I have puzzled for a long time as to how and when Arthur and Gay met. I have still not reached any positive conclusion. Arthur is listed in a very old address book of Gay's. His address is nearby her family home and at this time he is assistant editor of Amateur Gardening, while she is living and teaching in Nottingham. My first assumption was that they met through the Plymouth Brethren Chapel. As a child I understood that both families belonged to the Brethren. A letter from an old family friend dispels this supposition. She states that it was Gay's family who were Brethren; Arthur's were not. She says quite simply that Gay wanted to marry Arthur and he wanted to marry Gay. Gay was ostracised from her family to a large extent for the rest of her life. In a chapter about Arthur in *'Thoughtful Gardening'* by Robin Lane Fox, Robin alludes to the fact that, *'For a while, in his youth, he had inclined to the sect of Jehovah's Witnesses, a group he abandoned only with difficulty'.* This was a situation I was never aware of. Arthur remarked to Robin - after he published a book on ancient religion - *'. . . how fearful he had remained of his former sect'.*

Gay's father, Ebenezer Zamora Bolt, was a horticultural sundriesman at the time of their marriage. He could have been present at the same shows that Arthur the nurseryman or Arthur the journalist attended. There is a further possibility that Gay the botanist went to the same shows. One interesting fact that I came across is a link between Ebenezer and the British Carnation Society. At the time of writing the BCS are investigating this link for me. In an article in Commercial Horticulture there is a further link with the John Innes Horticultural Institution in Merton, London where Gay studied for a while. There is little doubt in my mind that they moved in the same circles.

Arthur and Gay married at Romford Register Office on 18 January 1933. Arthur's address is still nearby the Bolt family home. Gay's is in Sutton-in-Ashfield. Their first home was at Merton Park. Their honeymoon was spent with Arthur working with Macself, compiling *'The Gardener's Enquire Within'*, from articles taken from previous Amateur Gardening magazines, to be presented as a special offer for their Jubilee edition. Knowing Gay as well as I did I don't suppose she minded in the least. The following year they were looking for a small piece of land to extend their garden to grow more vegetables and the lilies that Gay loved, and to build a shack for weekend escapes. In those days the further south you went the more land you got for your money.

They found a six acre piece of scrubland full of brambles, willow scrub and long grass that had not been cultivated for over fifty years, with access only available from the bottom of the south facing slope, across a strip of land they didn't own. Gay the botanist fell in love with it. Arthur is reputed to have said, '*If you think I am making a garden here you've another think coming.*' At the bottom of this slope they built a wooden shack. They bought the two acre strip of land

27

over which they had access in 1937. The original wooden shed - with a lean-to on either side for goats - is long gone but a further wooden building stood on the same concrete base. On this same level a gang of workmen sunk a well, the water was analysed and approved by the local water authority in 1939 as *'fit for human consumption'*. This was their only source of water. Water for the livestock and the house they would build was pumped into a tank on the back of an old shooting brake and driven up the brick drive they had laid.

They lived in this shack at the weekends whilst building the house. This they did with the occasional help of friends. At that time sectional buildings were being sold through magazines, but Gay felt that something more substantial could be achieved if they built it themselves. With the aid of a couple of books, (still in my possession), Gay drew up plans based on the design of a Canadian barn and work commenced. It was finished before the beginning of the Second World War. There was no electricity or mains water. From January 1936 to July 1939 Gay undertook part time and or supply teaching, mainly at Surbiton High School (school certificate and sixth-form classes) and at

Parliament Hill School in Camden. I had thought that they moved directly from Merton Park to Rowfant. This I now know not to be so. In 1938 they were living in EC1 prior to moving to Orchards. All the original local council papers refer to a property known as 'Orchards Bungalow'. It is later that the property becomes known as 'The Orchards'.

I have a letter from one friend who helped with the building of the house. He remembered mixing concrete for the paths and sawing rafters to fit. In another letter, from a lady who worked for Arthur and Gay in the late forties and early fifties; she remembers, when aged eight or nine, meeting Gay as she and a friend were passing by a wooden storage building in the top right corner of the plot. Gay was measuring out chicken feed on scales, putting the measured grain into a wheelbarrow and marching off to feed the hens. Gay invited the girls to weigh some until she returned, which they did. They went away that day with eggs as their 'payment'. She returned with and without her friend many times to do small chores until, as a young woman she looked after us children from babyhood until 1953.

It has been written that the house was originally planned to be sited at the top of the slope where the land flattens out. I no longer believe this to be true either. In my archive the original site plan shows the house exactly where it was built, nearby an existing council sewer. If they had intended to build at the top of the slope initially; it could have been changed for two reasons. Firstly, in those exposed days of 1934, they feared they could be overlooked by the two small cottages built on the other side of the north boundary and secondly when they began the footings they came across a sandstone shelf.

It was also told that a specimen *Cedrus deodara* had been planted further down the slope to frame the view from the house. Now it sat on the west lawn. If the 1949 extension had not been built there would have been plenty of room for this delightful tree to mature. It must have given years of pleasure to my parents; certainly as small children we played beneath it. Many photographs show me as a small child, holding a kitten, dwarfed by this cedar. It was a very structural tree even as a young specimen, with its lovely bright delicate light green, soft young foliage, and its dreamy shape like a lady in flowing chiffon skirt; but then it began to grow, reaching upwards and outwards until by the 1980s the tips of some branches touched the lounge window. Sandstone was still present in this area and any large pieces dug out whilst digging the footings were laid to one side to be used later. The sandstone walls at Orchards were made from these stones.

The earliest photographs that I have show the house completed in 1938 as a 'two up, two down', with a galley kitchen and downstairs bathroom. Council papers, dated 1939, refer to the first rates as being due. This modest wooden home was made of Canadian cedar with cedar shingle roof tiles. The house had two further extensions; the first in 1949 giving a further bedroom and the 'Best Room' (lounge) as it was called. Both of these rooms had a fireplace and a wide mantelpiece made of West Hoathly brick, a particularly lovely brick with a purple hue and a bluish brick-red. The west elevation of this extension was brick built with the front and back clad in wood to match the original house. The second extension was built in 1959 to enlarge the kitchen and to make a study for Arthur and another bathroom upstairs. This extension was built entirely of brick.

Possibly because of the outbreak of war in September 1939 Arthur and Gay made the decision to move permanently to Rowfant. During and after the war, the land at Orchards was run as a market garden. In the late 1930s, apple, pear, plum and cherry orchards were planted, along with a large fruit garden containing red, black and white currants, black and white gooseberry bushes, raspberry and strawberry beds, a small grove of nut bushes and a large vegetable garden. Goats, cows, chickens and ducks were also kept. Gay also bred large white rabbits for their meat. Several land girls helped throughout this period, a couple of whom continued to work for Gay and Arthur for sometime after the war. Arthur still travelled to his office in London. During the war Arthur was in the Home Guard and was in charge of blowing up the local government petrol dump in Rowfant if the Germans ever invaded.

Arthur and Gay both wrote wartime books - Arthur's book was called *'War-Time Gardening for Home Needs'* detailing all that was needed to grow crops. Gay's book *'Utilising Wartime Crops for Home Needs'*, was a companion to Arthur's, giving advice on diet, storing and using vegetables, fruit and ancient and modern methods for preserving. Recipes for pickles, chutneys, jam, jelly and fruit syrups are also included. There is no publication date on either of these books. Arthur wrote a further book in 1949, when rationing was still in place *'Utility gardens for Home Needs'*. A couple of passages of text from this book were used in Jaqueline Mitchell's *'The Austerity Book'* published in early 2011. Arthur would have smiled broadly at his advice being reproduced some sixty years later still holding the same relevance.

In the 1950s I remember punnets of fruit being picked late in the evening and early in the morning and then delivered to Coopers the greengrocers in Horley, before Arthur caught the train to London. They also sold fresh cut daffodils to the local nursery Warrens. Sacks of named daffodil varieties had been bought from Covent Garden market in the 1930s and planted in large groups covering the front vista; along with the original sweep of wild daffodil that flowered in the rough grass. Many years later Gay had a passion for some of the more modern double forms and the new peachy and pinkish trumpet varieties. No concise records have been found but it is obvious from old black and white photographs that a shelter belt was planted on the north and west boundaries. It is within this shelter belt that the majority of the camellias now flourished.

As his career developed Arthur was a regular contributor for the Financial Times, Homes & Gardens, Country Life, the RHS journal 'The Garden', as well as writing for other magazines. Gay also wrote the occasional article for 'The Garden'. She was a partner in all his work. His professionalism in photography matched his professionalism in writing. Every journey he undertook whether in United Kingdom or abroad provided Arthur with another article, material for a lecture or contributed to a book. Now his own photographs were used to illustrate both. In 1966 with retirement imminent he was asked by Cramphorn Limited to become their Horticultural Consultant: he accepted. After Arthur's retirement, he travelled with Gay around Britain and Ireland and worldwide. They took their own caravan when undertaking the British and Irish tour. The product of this tour was the compilation of *'The Shell Guide to Gardens open to the Public'* first published in 1977.

In the early 1960s Arthur inherited his uncle's property in Jersey. Once they retired it was their wish to live there; however Arthur did not want to retire from writing. They came to realise that should Arthur continue to write and they lived in Jersey, the tax implications for them would be unsatisfactory. Then in 1971 they became grandparents. This also had a bearing on their future and retiring to Jersey became a dream. The Jersey house had already been divided into two flats which were rented out. Another of Gay's gems was to design a modest residence incorporating the existing garage. A later extension developed this into a substantial home. This became a holiday home for family and friends. From their travels, Gay introduced lots of bulbs and other plants to the already established garden. She also grew many more *Fuchsias* which were not reliably hardy in their garden at Orchards. *Fuchsias* were another of her passions.

1967 was the year of Arthur's retirement and also the year for his greatest accolade. Her Majesty the Queen awarded him an MBE for his services to horticulture and he received the Victoria Medal of Honour from the RHS; only sixty-three people in the horticultural world ever hold this medal at one time. A further tribute from the RHS was to feature a picture of Arthur on the front cover of their journal 'The Garden' in honour of his eightieth birthday in 1983. At that time the only other portrait featured was that of HRH Queen Elizabeth the Queen Mother.

In Jersey he and Gay were on several committees and they both consulted on and identified trees in many of the large manor house gardens, a number of which were featured in Country Life Magazine. At this time they met the late Violet Lort-Phillips, this lead to them advising on, sourcing and providing some of the magnificent trees that still stand in the Gerald Durrell Zoo in Trinity.

The Hardy Plant Society

Long before the Hardy Plant Society (HPS) was formed there was a National Hardy Plant Society. Arthur's future boss A J Macself chaired a meeting on 17 August 1910 where he explained the aims and aspects of the society. Representatives from several of the large nurseries attended including James C House of Isaac House & Sons, who was to be Arthur's employer in 1921. This meeting, held at The George Hotel Shrewsbury, was followed by the first meeting of the society at the Royal Caledonian Horticultural Society's Show on 7 September 1910. However the society was short-lived. Another attempt was made in the 1950s to form a HPS when the Delphinium Society was in difficulties.

In 1956 a meeting took place at Orchards at the late Alan Bloom's instigation. The late Will Ingwersen and the late John Sambrook also attended. This gathering led to an inaugural meeting chaired by Arthur; held at the RHS New Hall, Vincent Square, London, on 5 March 1957 and was attended by thirty people. They discussed the forming of the HPS. The first chairman was Alan Bloom and Arthur was on the first committee.

Arthur helped in many charitable ways - he was on the committee of The Gardener's Royal Benevolent Society (now called Perennial). An article he wrote about the charity led Colonel Furness to bequeath his home to the charity. Arthur is also credited with increasing donations to various charities following his articles.

September 1992

I don't remember the exact date but I know it was a Saturday. A call came from Arthur in the early evening asking me to come and look at his legs. Both were very swollen and turgid, his toes were blue and so were his lips. I took his freezing hands in mine. The doctor came quickly: gave him some medication and took me outside. 'He has fluid around his heart, he could die at any time or he could live for a week, a month who knows.' And so began the swift decline of Arthur.

When you see a face most days of your life, you don't really notice the changes that others might, but on reflection when I sifted through the most recent photographs of him, the differences were evident. A photograph taken earlier that month for the December edition of Country Life, when Arthur was featured on the frontispiece for his ninetieth birthday, shows the slight drop of one side of his face. I knew he was already having small Ischaemic strokes. By Christmas he had been in and out of hospital several times, back to live with me (when he started to write again) and then back to hospital. Immediately after the festive period I was asked to move him. Red Oaks the Gardeners' Royal Benevolent Home in Henfield, Sussex, was the obvious choice. I followed the ambulance that took him from the hospital in East Grinstead to Henfield; settled him in and signed all the necessary papers.

28 January 1993

Arthur died in Red Oaks less than a month later. He had not left his room since being admitted.

I visited him every day, sometimes with my husband Philip, sometimes with Iris Baker (an old family friend), once with my brother Edward. Edward found Arthur's condition too distressing to witness, so didn't come again. Matron suggested that the visits from me were not necessary; after all he was barely aware that I was there, she said. To Iris she questioned whether I realised that he was going to die. 'Of course', Iris replied.

But I continued my visits, stayed for an hour and drove home. I would tell him about his garden, what was flowering, what was looking good, talk to him about his grandchildren. I read him poetry and talked about Gay. He had a calmness and serenity about him; an acceptance. He would turn his now glazed blue eyes to me and still they smiled. But he said not a word. I held his thin, cold fingers in my hand. A whisper of a grip passed from his to mine. He knew I was there.

Matron had been instructed to call me at any time, day or night, if she knew his time was close. The call came at 9am, within minutes I was on the road. I collected Iris on the way. Together we sat hour after hour, whilst his breathing became more laboured. The nurses would come and turn him at intervals, until eventually I asked them to leave him so he was facing me. I sat holding his hand and stroking his brow and talking about Gay. I thanked him for all he had ever done for me but told him that Gay was waiting for him. I kissed his forehead; the breaths became more shallow and rasping, with more time in between each. Iris spoke. 'Goodbye Mr Hellyer' and to me 'It's nearly time.' And then there was silence. Almost on cue the nurses entered the room. I bent forward and kissed him once more. The time was 2.20pm.

Where does that strength come from? When your heart is broken? When the man, who has been your rock for forty-five years, has gone? Was it the knowledge that I had carried out Gay's wishes and looked to him until the end? A promise I made her many years before her death, when she worried so much as to what would become of him, should she pass first. Maybe the strength came from the help I had given him in his last months, writing letters on his behalf, to the various magazines awaiting articles from him. Possibly it was from the love and care I was able to give once again; when he needed it the most.

Within moments I was sitting in Matron's office discussing what I had to do next, more papers to sign, telephone calls to make. I drove Iris home with me. Together we went to see Edward. Iris stayed with him and I returned home to make calls to all the important people in Arthur's life. I sat at my telephone and waded through Arthur's address book, ringing the people I ought to tell before a report of his death hit the news. It was during a conversation with Robin Lane Fox that I committed myself to opening Arthur's garden. But it was later when reading so many of the letters of condolence and his obituaries that I realised just how well thought of Arthur had been. Several spoke of the 'wide influence' that many of his articles had, as well as his books. To me he was just my daddy.

Chapter Two

Grace Charlotte Hellyer BSc

Grace Charlotte Hellyer née Bolt was the first daughter of Ebenezer Zamora Bolt and his wife Charlotte Elizabeth née French. She was born at the family home, 47 Oakfield Road, Seven Kings, Essex on 9 March 1907. Her father was a horticultural sundriesman. From the books that I still own from her childhood onwards; I am sure her parents encouraged and enriched her life on a diverse range of subjects, including poetry, botany and literature; at the age of seven her father gave her a First Aid Book. She was, I think, a very bright and industrious child. From an early age she was called Gracie and then Gay. This name she was to use for the rest of her life. No photographs remain of Gay as a youngster. One picture I have shows a family group, the only ones I recognise are Gay, Arthur and my maternal grandmother.

She was an intellectual and academic student. She studied at Ilford County High School, Essex from 1918 to 1925 gaining nine credits and one distinction in Chemistry and Pure Maths. From there she went to University of London Birkbeck College for a year to study Zoology, then to Bedford College as a resident for three years, studying Botany, Zoology and Chemistry. In 1930 she gained her Teachers Training Diploma from Kings College. During this time she had glowing references written for her, when hoping to be chosen for a Herman Frasch Fellowship at Cornell University. Letters of recommendation, written for her later that year for the teaching position she was applying for in Nottingham, made it clear that she was not successful but the comments were just as compelling. All Gay's professors viewed her as studious, keen, conscientious and high principled, enjoying student life with zest and delight. Gay's talent for drawing was a great asset for her scientific work. Her many interests did not detract from her work, which was always paramount. She was a member of the boating, walking and country dancing clubs.

Gay's first teaching position in 1930 was at Sutton-in-Ashfield County Secondary School in Nottingham. Prior to her appointment biology had not been taught at the school. Her first task was to completely reorganise the science department, bringing it up to date. The course she taught included field work, gardening and the academic work needed for the School Certificate and Higher Certificate examinations. The girls were stimulated by her teaching methods and took an enthusiastic interest in the subject. In 1936, four years after her departure, the course she initiated was still being used. She left in December 1932 to marry Arthur.

Several specialist courses were also undertaken - the dates for these are unknown. Gay attended Imperial College for Plant Pathology. Plymouth Marine

Biological Station - marine biology and at John Innes Horticultural Institution taking a post graduate, genetics and cytology course.

In the early days of their marriage it is obvious that Gay worked alongside Arthur in all things, drawing plans and assisting with the building of their house; (I still have her hand written diagram for the wiring at Orchards), working the land during the war alongside the land girls; planning the orchards, helping with the animals until she finally returned to teaching at the local grammar school where she taught Zoology, Botany and Biology from 1949 until 1963 when she retired.

In 2003, I made contact with several of her students during her time at East Grinstead Grammar School. They all spoke very highly of her. Dennis Minson was one of her first students. He described Gay's arrival as being like a *'spring breeze'*, very different from anything he had previously experienced. Some of the students' practical work was carried out at Orchards over the next few years. Minson graduated and worked at the Grassland Research Institute near Henley where he gained a PhD. Then followed a year in Ottawa, before working in New Zealand for two years. From there he took a permanent job working on tropical grasses in Australia. Following his retirement in 1993 he returned with his wife to live in England. His name was very familiar to me, as he had kept in regular contact with Gay. In 1994 he drove along the farm lane, slowing at our drive; despite the years that had gone by I recognised him. We had tea under the oak tree where Gay's ashes were interred, whilst I filled him in on the last thirty years and all our future plans for the garden. He wrote to me later, '*I left our meeting enthralled and so excited at renewing my association with the Hellyer family and their garden.*'

Peter Freeland has furnished me with a lot of information regarding Gay's time at the grammar school where she taught him. During her lunch hour she supplied some students with the additional information that they would need for Agricultural Science which was an O-level subject in 1955-7. Her pupils referred to her as 'Mrs H' which he says; '*Was almost a courtesy title considering some of the other members of staff were given fairly unpleasant nicknames.*' She had a particular way of teaching which boded well with her pupils (she was the same with us children too). She would never give you a

46

direct answer to a question, encouraging you to seek the answer in the relevant book. She wanted you to read, understand, digest and commit to memory all the factual details of importance. Much of the time in their classes was taken up with informal chatting. Peter found this frustrating at the time, however he now realises that she had two objectives. The first was to discover as much as possible about each of her students. The second was to introduce areas of biology that might stimulate interest and broaden their horizons. She was a great encourager. She organized sixth form outings during the school holidays to different London venues, accompanying her pupils on a bus or train. They all went on to have distinguished and illustrious careers and all the ex-pupils that I made contact with, remembered her with a good deal of affection fifty years later.

My memory of her is someone who was severely lamed by arthritis. She took to greenhouse gardening. Her cedar greenhouse and south facing veranda were filled with an eclectic mix of houseplants and bulbs. She grew *Crocus, Hyacinths, Freesias, paperwhite Narcissus, Lachenalia,* soft leaved *Campanula, Calceolaria,* and *Coleus* to name but a few. In the

47

'Best Room' houseplants were suspended either side of a long white extendable plant pole - wedged between ceiling and floor - in rings of plastic coated metal, two plants per plastic ellipse. This was ideal for plants with a trailing habit. I remember the thick fabric-like petals of a pale pink *Hoya* dripping sweet nectar to the cork parquet floor beneath. Larger houseplants were placed in saucers around the base, in a vain attempt to conceal the pole.

Saintpaulias sat in ceramic dishes on a small side table. Other plants were placed on hydroculture pellets in a 'table conservatory'. This large transparent plastic 'drum', which clipped into a plastic tray, stood in the corner near the window; the plastic lid had a central circular vent with holes in, that could be turned to increase or decrease ventilation. It was planted up with ferns and other moisture loving plants. It was far too large to be on a table. Gay became an expert in this field and this led her to write *'Indoor Gardening Made Easy'*. She wrote another slim book *'Growing your own Vegetables'* both published in 1976.

In the late sixties and early seventies all the vegetables and fruit that Arthur grew she used. Sitting at her oak table (which I still own), she would slice runner beans, shell peas; prepare apples, gooseberries, strawberries, currants and pears, freezing enough for her family and her grandchildren. Gay's input was just as important as Arthur's. The vegetable season ended with Gay and me making copious amounts of green tomato chutney. All the main ingredients were sourced from the garden. This recipe I still use today; although I make far less, but it is still much enjoyed by my family and my new Italian family.

After my marriage in 1967, Gay and I became great friends. I lived with my family, within the garden in what had been the 'service' bungalow. Despite her lameness we would walk around the garden on most days when she wasn't travelling. Every November on my birthday she would walk alone, picking me anything that was in flower or of interest - the little posy always contained *Viburnum fragrans*. She encouraged me to observe the buds in winter, the unfurling leaves in spring, and the tiny flowers on some of the shrubs, to take in their fragrance and later in the year to take note of the difference in the foliage and the berries that had formed. We felt the texture of the leaves, *Stachys byzantina* being one of the softest; aptly named 'Lamb's Ears'. They reminded me of a time when, as a child, we helped bottle-feed lambs shunned by their mothers at the nearby farm. Their silky ears a smooth contrast to their bouncy rugged coats. We looked underneath at the downy backs of *Magnolia grandiflora*; in later years we walked with my daughters and she would educate them also. We had many poisonous trees in the garden, she metered out the same rules as she had done to me. 'Never pick anything in the garden without permission. Never eat anything unless you ask first.' The rule was broken by my eldest daughter, who I found under the mulberry tree picking and eating raspberry-coloured berries. She was very sick that evening and on into the night - the mulberry is ripe only when almost as dark as a blackberry. She didn't touch any kind of berry for many years.

Gay was a wonderful grandmother, both strict and indulgent in equal measure. She made practical Viyella nightdresses, which lasted from babyhood to eighteen months. A simple caftan style with a round neck, three pleats hand sewn across the shoulders down to just above the waistline which could be unpicked as the child grew. The sleeves had a simple cotton ribbon sewn near the wrist. When baby was small the ribbon was tied over the little hands, so she could move about but not scratch herself, when older tied around the wrist to make it snug. The bottom edge was also pleated three times, so as the child grew, the length could be altered. She also knitted shawls, cardigans and little jumpers. She pulled the horsehair from an old mattress, washed it thoroughly and made a horsehair mattress covered in good quality ticking to replace the modern sponge one in the carry cot and a further one for the pram. She also knitted for other family members making a 'Brighton Tigers' jumper for Arthur to wear to the Sunday ice hockey matches. Her other hobby was rug making, both with a pattern and without. Her masterpiece - to my mind - was a blue-bordered herbaceous garden rug which she made on the dining room table. When she had completed the first half, she made another, a mirror image of the first and sewed it together. This was for their Jersey home. The girls loved her dearly. The nickname she gave to my youngest daughter 'Saucy-Charlie' is still used. Despite an arthritic hip she would be on her hands and knees playing with them and after her hip operation in January 1977 she allowed them to crawl all over her bed.

11 February 1977

I woke with a start, fully conscious; no drowsy eyes and yawning away the last of sleep; the time 5.50am. The girls were silent in the room next door. Gay's smile filled my subconscious, she winked her green eye and mouthed goodbye. The telephone rang. The time was 5.55am. I fell out of bed, in eight strides for the normal dozen or so steps; I grabbed the telephone from the shelf in the hall. The girls still slept. The hairs on my arms and neck stood up and an involuntary shiver ran through my body. 'Penny,' said Arthur softly, 'Penny, can you come? I think Gay is dead.' I knew it. My skin crept, goosebumps rose from my skin. I knew it when I woke five minutes earlier. The girls' father slept soundly neither disturbed by my rapid exit from bed or from the trills of the telephone. Little voices called as I clambered into my track suit and socks. Quietly I explained that mummy had to go to see granddad urgently, that daddy would get them ready for school today and that I wouldn't be long. Shaking their father into a semi-conscious state I whispered with urgency the information; he dozed once more. I shook him again instructing him to say nothing to the girls and to please make them breakfast.

I was at Arthur's front door and up the stairs by 6am. There she sat, slumped against the bathroom wall, her pretty curls in slight disorder, her white nightdress covering her dignity. I flew to his telephone and called the doctor. Running to her bedroom I grabbed her duvet, covering her with it. She was still warm and so, so soft. 'She's dead, no need to keep her warm' said Arthur.

Because her death had occurred at home the police were called. As she had only been home from hospital for a few days following a hip replacement operation; a Coroners Inquest was required. The family were divided about the next course of action to be taken. I was also clear in my mind that however painful the family may find it, we had to follow her desires; and so by the end of that day her corneas had saved the sight of two people. The agonising wait for the inquest added pressure to a bereft Arthur. The verdict - misadventure. Again the family were divided. I persuaded Arthur that no amount of compensation would bring Gay back and in truth he knew, that it would make very little difference to the neglect that had clearly played a part in her untimely death. After her cremation her final wish was carried out and she was laid to rest forever; at

Orchards. It was several years later that Arthur was to tell me how grateful he was that I had insisted that he should adhere to her wishes.

Chapter Three

Working the land

Arthur & Gay

They were both a bit of a mystery to me, as many parents are to their children, but to me, even more so, as I was adopted. In 1947 they adopted two baby boys who were not related, who they named Edward and Peter. Although first fostered in 1949, they later adopted me in the early 1950s. In fact it was for this reason that the first extension to the house was built.

Details of how they met and their subsequent marriage were never discussed and no wedding photographs are in the collection that I still own. Gay told me that she was married in a green satin evening dress; a dress I was to find in the back of a cupboard thirty years after she died. She did tell me about how little money they managed on and how if they had six old pence left at the end of the week they would treat themselves to a seat up in the 'gods' at the theatre or cinema.

Arthur's father had died two decades before I was born; his mother lived a sick-rendering car journey away in Bristol with two spinster sisters-in-law. We met maybe twice a year. These visits were looked forward to with dread and fascination. They all appeared to be so aged; which of course they were. Arthur was forty-seven years old when I was fostered before my adoption. We sat in a room full of Victorian nostalgia - stuffed birds in glass cases, out of reach on top of glass-fronted bookcases; deep green velvet curtains hung from large sash windows; elegant furniture surrounded us. I remember being intrigued by an elegant black sculptured hand used as a paperweight.

Gay's father died the year after my birth. Although Gay's mother lived until the age of ninety-four we had no regular contact and no input from the family as many other families would have done.

I think as children we all absorbed something different from the garden at Orchards. For Edward it was the joy of new machines being sent to Arthur for trial. He was the one who became most excited, wanting to try it as soon as it was put together. Cutting the grass was his main job. Peter spent much of his time at boarding school, but his greatest love was bird watching and rough shooting. As children we led an idyllic life. We still had goats, ducks and chicken. One of my jobs was to unlock the ducks from the triangle-shaped arc - as a youngster I was very nervous as they quacked, flapped, rushed and stumbled over each other in their anticipation to be first down the ramp. We had the freedom to roam as far as we liked. We made camps, climbed trees, rode our bikes up and down the garden. We played football on a 'pitch' behind the old sheds. When we were older we learnt to drive on the top grass - then called the racing track - in Arthur's dark green mini.

With Gay's return to teaching, at the local grammar school in 1949, the need for a childminder and some domestic help became more important. A bungalow was built in the early 1950s in the top corner of the property. The bungalow was designed by Gay and built in brick by local builders. It was detached, facing south with a view of one of the original apple orchards planted in the early thirties. A cherry orchard was removed to facilitate this building. The farm lane ran alongside the east boundary. The north facing kitchen overlooked a rose garden filled with one variety of a thornless, pale peachy-pink non-fragrant rose. A large expanse of lawn ran up towards the back boundary, which was planted with a narrow shelter belt of native trees, originally planted to protect the young cherry trees. A row of six tall poplars planted on the west side of the grass gave some kind of boundary and protection. One very mature common oak, a weeping mulberry and two large fruiting cherries were the only other trees nearby.

The first family to live there were from Hythe in Kent. Iris Baker was at that time already a mother of four boys, one of whom I am still in close contact with; two more babies arrived in later years; her only daughter is also still in contact with me. Cyril her husband worked as a fireman at The Beehive at Gatwick (the original Gatwick airport). During this period he worked for several hours a week in the garden at Orchards. His main duty was to cut the grass, while

Iris worked as a domestic in the main house. She found Gay a hard taskmaster and within a few years they decided to move to a council house in Horley. I remember sitting on the stairs listening to this conversation and then crying myself to sleep. My relationship with Iris spanned more than five decades, until her death in 2008. It was during their time at Orchards that the last of the chickens went - attacked by the Baker's dog Spot.

They were the only 'service folk' to live in the bungalow. Professional people then rented it; and briefly in 1965 it was put on the market and then withdrawn. When the Bakers left, Jean Williams, an ex-land girl who worked at Orchards during the war travelled from East Grinstead several days a week to do the domestic work. Arthur tackled the garden for several years almost single-handed.

Planting, gardening maintenance, turf laying and other horticultural photographs were taken in the garden at the bungalow and the greenhouses at Orchards. They were used in Amateur Gardening magazine and in Arthur's books. I remember those days with affection - Peter Ayres the photographer and

Brian Walkden who 'stage-managed' the photographs; were very friendly and kind.

In 1968, some months after my marriage we moved into the service bungalow. The garden still had no defined boundaries, being part of the garden at Orchards. A narrow concrete path lead from the rustic garden gate, to wide curved brick built steps that took you up to a straight concrete path to the front porch. Narrow borders edged the two square lawns on three sides; traditional garden design of the 1950s. On one side of the garden path; a low brick wall, on the other a rose garden filled with new cultivars and seedling roses given to Arthur by various growers. The couch grass in this border caused constant problems. The outer edges of these lawns were bordered and supported by low sandstone walls. A clipped specimen of boxwood was placed atop the steps on either side of the path. Below the retaining wall a further narrow bed was planted with *Fuchsia*s grown by Gay.

The narrow borders against the bungalow contained no more than *Cotoneaster horizontalis*, *Lonicera periclymenum* 'Belgia' and a large flowered orangey-scarlet *Chaenomeles*; complimented by daffodils in the spring and sedums for the summer. Over the retaining wall, different shades of purple *Aubrietia* and *Iberis* trailed. A wider border on the west of the bungalow was filled with *Lonicera periclymenum* 'Serotina', *Viburnum davidii, Hypericum* 'Hidcote' and *Pernettya* now called *Gaultheria*, covered with bright purple, white and palest pink berries on the different plants. On the east side of the bungalow in the shelter of the two remaining cherry trees; a wonderful *Hedera canariensis* 'Gloire de Marengo' clambered up the brickwork, with a bank of pink mop head *Hydrangeas* at its feet.

For my twenty-fourth birthday Gay and Arthur gave me a greenhouse. Maybe they were tired of me taking over theirs. I had developed a keen interest in propagation, using either Gay's cedar greenhouse, for the most part a little too warm and damp, because this is where she grew some of her houseplants, or Arthur's part brick sunken greenhouse: my favourite. The aluminium top was a replacement to the original but the brick walls were Arthur's handiwork from the 1940s. A concrete path led down into the greenhouse, cemented walls on either side afforded adequate depth of soil for his tomato plants in the summer and exactly the correct height for tending seedlings etc. It was fitted out with water systems and electricity. Now with a greenhouse of my own all I pinched were flowerpots!

My greenhouse was a 'glass to ground span-roofed' aluminium structure, filled in the summer months with early lettuces grown amongst tomatoes, melons and Chinese lantern - *Physalis alkekengi* - usually grown for indoor winter decoration, either dried with its orange-red calyx or picked when faded beige and skeletonised. The red berry held within is edible with a somewhat acidic but pleasant flavour if the fruit is fully ripe. It can be eaten fresh or made into sauces or preserves. I grew it in the greenhouse in the hope that the fruits would ripen fully. Used in the garden border it made a run in all directions with new shoots popping up where you least expected them. The staging on the other side was filled with a diverse selection of vegetable and annual seedlings and cuttings of herbaceous and shrubs from the garden. It became an escape from a troubled marriage. My space; where my youngest daughter drew her first picture for me, on the back of a polystyrene meat tray. We would sit on many rainy afternoons in the greenhouse, I would potter, tell her stories, she was happy just to be in my company.

Gay gave me a copy of her book *'Growing your own Vegetables'* with a message inside *'now you try'*. Although I already grew vegetables, at this stage my outlook was 'lazy and haphazard'. My reasons - or were they excuses? - were many. With a young family devoting sufficient time to garden was difficult. Moments were caught between naps, feeds and all the other domestic clutter of life and when my youngest was two years old, a morning job at the local nursery - unfortunately not a plant nursery but a toddler one; although I did sell plants there. Any reading would have been done in the evening but I did, and still do, fall asleep with a book if I am too comfortable. Another reason was ill health, eventually diagnosed as soft tissue arthritis, an autoimmune disorder along with a thyroid malfunction.

Gay had been my driving force; always the educator, keen to share her knowledge. I felt certain that my appreciation of plants was down to Gay not Arthur. He was always so busy either working in the garden, writing about it, editing, travelling, lecturing and judging. The only shrubby additions to the bungalow garden were three camellias given to me as a birthday present and hundreds of daffodil bulbs thinned from their Jersey garden. So much more fun planting with small children who took great delight in plugging the holes once the bulb was planted and stamping them down with their little feet.

A rough and ready swimming pool had been dug behind the house; this provided endless pleasure for us children including the boys that lived in the new bungalow. I remember a huge hole left (so we were told) by a German bomber offloading before its journey home. This was used as a dump for garden rubbish for many years. Gay later instructed that it should be further dug out and the removed soil built up around the edges. The enlarged rectangle was then shuttered and filled with concrete. For a long while, a scaffold pole was used as a hand rail as there were no steps. Later simple steps were installed. A strong wooded plank acted as a diving board. The pool had a shallow end sloping to the deepest part in the middle. It was not very long so any diving would have taken you to the deepest part.

Childhood gardening reminiscences

There are many memories from my childhood that will remain with me forever. The garden at Orchards was a wilderness you could lose yourself in. As a young child a weeping willow grew for many years directly down from the house. You could give the impression to all who may care, that you were walking to the outbuildings, once out of sight behind an evergreen *Berberis*, you could dodge and duck behind the many trees and shrubs and come back up the garden blocked from the view of the house. Many hours were spent under this tree as a child, to escape my warring brothers. The only companions who would find me there were my cats.

We made frequent trips to the RHS garden at Wisley. Arthur would be judging a trial and Gay would walk round with the children. I still have a picture of me at an early age running between the long herbaceous borders down from Battlestone Hill. We visited Great Dixter often. The late Christopher Lloyd was a friend and colleague of Arthur and Gay. It was Arthur who helped him be appointed to the staff of Country Life.

The beauty of the gardens of Milton Mount College, where I was at school for a few years, made the homesickness of being a boarder just bearable. The school building was a huge Victorian pile with a majestic Lebanon cedar hanging its canopy over a separate detached house where the head mistress lived.

In the grounds I recall a round pond, clipped yews, a ha-ha, broad curved stone steps and balustrades, a Dutch lawn and an enclosed *Camellia* walk curved in design, brick and glass in structure with a black and quarry tiled floor. Beyond the playing fields there was a maze which was strictly out of bounds. This was a favourite escape for half a dozen of us. When the school began to sell off some of the land, this part of the grounds was the first to go for housing development. To my horror one of my friends, a day girl lived in one of these new houses. Both of us were cross with her parents for a long time because we blamed them for losing us the maze. The school building is long gone, but the garden remains. Although some of it is altered from those days - much is exactly as I remember it. It is open to the public and although the block of flats, built in the place of the old building is ugly, the views they must have make up for the outside facade. The original stable block which in my day was the science laboratories does remain, now converted into a number of apartments.

We would walk to church on Sundays down a long avenue of beech trees catching falling leaves in the late autumn days. It was considered lucky to catch them before they fell to the ground. Not so lucky if you came out of the crocodile line in your effort to do so. As a punishment I was frequently given one hundred lines of - 'I must stay in line'. The avenue is still there; now houses line both sides, set back from the trees.

The Dutch lawn was the setting for summer plays. I was once a nymph in chiffon dress skipping barefoot from behind clipped yews. Those days were magical. Huge *Rhododendrons* and *Azaleas* surrounded the tennis courts; here we were shown how to suck the back of the flowers to gain the nectar within. I returned once just before the old school was demolished. The magic of the grounds had not gone. But the secret passages that led from the basements to either side of the steps leading to the round pond were no longer there.

My recollections are a patchwork of other fascinating places, whose beauty remains with me to this day. The wild ruggedness of the Isles of Scilly was enjoyed several times. I loved all the wild flowers. Peter enjoyed bird watching. We all enjoyed the boat trips from one island to another; the skippers quite often allowing us to take the helm. We visited Tresco gardens with its strange alien-looking plants; unfamiliar in those days to many gardens in England; even in the south. I remember I found many of the plants very bizarre. *Gladiolus byzantina* was growing wild in the hedgerows on St Mary's. It had been grown in the fields at some time for the cut flower market. I grew it at Orchards and still grow it in my garden in Italy.

In Jersey windswept trees bent awkwardly by the wind on the north of the island, stood starkly against the sky. The garden at Rockwood, originally the home of Arthur's Uncle Ernest was further developed by Gay and Arthur after he inherited it in the 1960s. Gay's passion for *Fuchsias* was exploited to the full. She was able to grow many different varieties because of the milder weather in Jersey. Tall hedges of *Fuchsia magellanica* surrounded many of the old cottages. Most vividly I remember the curtains of *Mesembryanthemum* hanging from the rocks and cliffs down to Portelet Bay, fleshy greyish-green leaves and bright fuchsia-pink daisy flowers.

The dunes in the St Ouen's area were edged with hare's tail, other tufted grasses and sea holly. Arthur's aunts' house at Grouville led directly to a rocky beach. Remarkably low tides exposed numerous rock pools; opening our young eyes to a new world of nature. Little shellfish, crabs, whelks, barnacles, limpets, winkles and gobies could all be found in the deep pools. My lasting memory from Grouville are the two green glazed terracotta jugs from Great Aunt Lily's garden - given to me for my twenty-first birthday; a gift I still have and admire.

The Isle of Skye; dramatic on the day we visited. I don't remember how old I was. Undulating roads edged for miles with heathers, wildness, waterfalls and a striking grey-black sky a backdrop to the red and black Cuillin Mountains that straddle the island. They are most famous for their rugged grandeur. To the east the red hills have a soft, rounded outline to their steep sides. To the west, hard jagged edges rise to nearly one thousand metres. They are a mix of gabbro (a dark, coarse-grained plutonic rock, consisting mainly of pyroxene, plagioclase feldspar and often olivine) and granite. So my love of nature remains from my earliest memories.

I know that I cherished the tranquillity of Orchards. I was only ever encouraged to pick daises and dandelions from the lawn. Gay felt that garden flowers should remain there - in the garden. Only on special occasions could I pick from the garden. Then the instructions continued. Daffodils should be picked as low down the stem as possible and snapped cleanly. Never remove leaves - these are needed to feed the bulb for the following years' flowers. Your secateurs should be clean when cutting branches from the shrubs. Gay would show exactly where to make the cut and the swiftness of it, so avoiding damage to the stem. When we helped with apple picking we were shown how to cup the apple in the palm of your hand and give a slight twist. If it was ripe it would come way gently. And we were never allowed to eat any but the windfalls; as the good apples picked from the trees were sold. Gay would look at the stalks and know that you had picked it from the tree. It was many years later that she was to show me how she knew. Maybe that is why I used to eat the entire apple - core and all - to destroy the evidence. One year I dug up a wild daffodil bulb from the farm lane for Mother's Day. Gay was far from impressed, not only because I had taken something that wasn't mine but also because the garden was already full of daffodils, both wild and cultivated. I was made to return the bulb to the place from which it had come.

Whilst growing up in this environment, I was not aware of the hard work that went into the creating or maintaining of the garden. Although we did various chores as children, it was not until after my first marriage that I took a keen interest in gardening. Arthur's garden was full of flowers and we had access to the entire garden. I remember then that I had a profound wish to be able to go into my garden, not his, and fill a vase for my home. Often I would walk through the top woodland and pick trusses of rhododendron to fill shallow containers for the house. Although Arthur and Gay grew enough fruit and vegetables for all of the family, I was encouraged to develop my own vegetable and fruit garden.

After Arthur's retirement in 1967 they set off on the next phase of their working life, in many ways this was possibly their busiest time. Gay dealt with the proofreading, botanical checks, indexing his books (a job I assisted in when Gay broke her wrist), indexing and filing his growing library of slides, as well as being his best friend and stalwart companion, travelling to Russia, America and South Africa; so that in retirement he could continue his career in a freelance capacity. She rarely, if ever, complained about the pain her arthritic hip gave her.

I went with Arthur to the RHS shows in London, in those early days after Gay's death. They had worked as

71

a very close team for ten years. His confidence was shattered. We talked endlessly as to what he should do. I said that, even though he was seventy-four, he should continue to work if that was what he wanted to do. This advice he took. For the first couple of years I visited him daily, cooked him lunch and did odd sewing jobs and worked with him in the garden. Together we moved many of the *Camellias* in the top northwest corner of the garden. He was worried about me digging; and I was worried about him doing the same. With great strength we pulled and tugged at one *Camellia* with an enormous root ball, with one final shove he almost buried me beneath it. Despite our grief we had great fun. This area became known as the *Camellia* Grove. This group were still planted too closely. Within this grove grew a *Styrax japonica*, the Japanese Snowbell, its tiny bell-shaped flowers hung delicately along the branches in spring, the glossy mid green leaves the perfect foil; then in autumn this greenness became an explosion of buttercup-yellow foliage. Nearby several *Acer palmatum* seedlings -one of which Arthur grew from seed - gave a vibrant contrast with their vivid red autumn colour. A specimen *Camellia* x *williamsii* 'J C Williams' was by then twelve feet tall. I remembered it from childhood, often one of the earliest to flower in its sheltered position. We developed a great companionship, but he could not bear for Gay's name to be mentioned.

It has often been discussed since their deaths, as to what Arthur and Gay's original intentions for Orchards had been. One suggestion that they intended to start their own lily nursery but found the soil to be unsuitable, I find difficult to believe. I now know, having researched a Garden Record book found amongst my old papers, that a great number of ornamental trees and shrubs were introduced with the fruit trees in 1935. In 1938 several roses were added. By 1939 the orchards were planted and in 1949 borders were created using shrubs and herbaceous plants. A steady planting of trees, shrubs and roses took place between 1950 and 1960. During the spring and autumn of 1952 *Rhododendrons* were purchased followed by twenty-seven more in 1958, further plantings being undertaken in 1971. In 1953 a huge number of *Camellias* were bought for the top northwest corner of the garden. In March 1955 Arthur bought a further thirty-six *Azaleas*, none named. I believe they were probably the *Azalea mollis* with yellow or orange flowers that filled the woodlands with heady scent. The list now researched is by no means complete. Hundreds more shrubs, roses and climbers were introduced by them both over the years.

Extended house - late 1940s/early 1950s

Part Two

Chapter One

Moving Down the Hill

A kind of madness led to my suggestion that Arthur and I should swap homes. It wasn't that simple it has to be said and the exact details will not be presented here but to all intents and purposes that is what we did. Arthur was looking for ways to leave the house at Orchards as it was too full of memories for him. He couldn't bear the loneliness; working just as hard and enjoying my company during the day, when we would garden together; his sadness at losing Gay was palpable. Once again he applied for conversion of the outbuildings into which he could have moved; this was refused. He talked of closing up the house and living elsewhere. On April Fools' Day we moved homes, just over thirteen months after Gay's death.

Now the garden at least around the house was my responsibility. It was my time to make my mark on this wonderful woodland setting - suddenly the energy and enthusiasm for the shrubs, the trees, the borders, rushed though me and was to stay with me for the next twenty-seven years. Now I had to read the books, identify the shrubs; search out the cultivation and pruning requirements. I had learnt a lot from my decade at the bungalow; where I'd made my own fruit and vegetable garden but that was just a minute part of the knowledge I was to learn.

There is a real need to understand your patch whatever the size. To work within it and with it. For whole days at a time if possible; and in different seasons. To follow the sun - note the length of the shadows cast and understand for yourself your chosen plants' needs. It is said that when taking over someone else's garden you should wait for one whole year before making any drastic decisions. Even though the garden was known to me I now began to observe many things previously ignored and realised my lack of knowledge of the general maintenance required.

Arthur continued to grow vegetables and fruit for a few years but with my busy life and no Gay to freeze for us all, much was wasted. Many years previously Arthur had extended the vegetable and fruit garden and planted *Thuya occidentalis* 'Rheingold' alternated with *Juniperus virginiana* 'Skyrocket'. We were never sure why he did this except that each was planted against one metal post of the cage from which netting would be draped if we were troubled by pigeon, blackbird or squirrel. Not that any protection made that much difference, the birds and animals found their way in and out quite easily. When the vegetable garden was disbanded Arthur replanted three of the 'Skyrocket' in a group and cut the rest for firewood. The 'Rheingold' trees were moved into a horseshoe shape. I think they both would have been amused to know that when the garden was open for the National Gardens Scheme, children would be found playing hide and seek around and through these specimens; their squeals of delight and excitement filling the air.

Gardening should be a pleasure not a chore. You can feel rewarded without following all the dictates of either the day or the current trends. To know the Latin name for the plants that grow in your garden is the first important step. From that you can find all the relevant advice. At that point you can choose to follow all the advice given or ignore some or even all of it. People may think you are showing off by learning the Latin names, but early on I found that one common name for a plant could be completely different in another region.

Unlike so many gardens we did not have a wall or fence to mark the end of the garden abruptly. The area was so large that from the house; which was almost central in the plot, the eye would go on forever across ancient woodland to the distant horizon. On the eastern side of the plot an impenetrable hedge of *Rosa rugosa* had been planted in the 1930s to keep out the farmer's cattle; which were driven twice daily along the farm lane. The other original boundaries were simple post and wire fencing along the south and native hedging on the north and west side. Later neglect transformed this into an open boundary of leggy trees; occasionally layered if the growth was of hazel or infilled with branch debris.

Arthur in the Bungalow

Arthur was seventy-five years old. The move to the bungalow not too dramatic as it was still within his garden and he could see the sense of his grandchildren having more room to grow. He didn't let the bungalow garden stand still either. The rustic structures that had supported the climbing roses were replaced with brick pillars which he laid himself, with supports of thick timber between each pillar. The narrow garden which ran beneath the pergola was extended on the west side. A mix of *Mahonia*, *Acers*, *Philadelphus* and herbaceous plants filled this area, affording Arthur a colourful view from the kitchen window. My vegetable garden disappeared under completely new planting of interesting trees and shrubs, with a modest herbaceous border near the house. *Paulownia tomentosa* - the Foxglove tree - a tree I had never seen until then - flowered upright panicles of fragrant pinkish-lilac flowers marked purple and yellow inside, in the spring. Twelve inch light green leaves followed. *Sorbus aria* 'Lutescens', the early foliage silvery-grey aging to grey-green carried white spring flowers which were followed by brown-speckled dark red berries. This cultivar of *Sorbus* was one of the first trees I planted down the hill nearby the lime green of *Robinia pseudoacacia* 'Frisia'. Once again the garden was transformed.

A study was built in the attic of the bungalow with a large window overlooking one of the original orchards. Much of the garden was hidden from his view by an ancient oak tree and a tall larch, up which Arthur had planted many years before, an unnamed scrambling rose, which now cascaded from the top. Small clusters of single, white, yellow-stamened flowers billowed from the long stems, sweet fragrance swept into the window to the table where he worked. Arthur had used the same table in his study at Orchards. A solid rectangular oak writing table, covered with red leatherette with two drawers either side. These drawers held his writing paraphernalia. One drawer left open for his small ginger cat 'Tom'; who would curl up for a sleep whilst Arthur worked.

For the most part Arthur looked after himself, undertaking most of the domestic chores whilst continuing to work, write, travel, photograph and judge. Edward took early retirement to become his companion and driver. They both continued to work in the garden.

Restoring the Neglect

The garden in general, but particularly around the main house, showed neglect from earlier years. The borders were full of *Aegopodium podagraria* - Ground Elder. A pot-herb and medicine thought to have been introduced by the Romans; it was used against rheumatism and gout. I think one of its common names is very apt - Garden Plague. It had invaded the garden in a similar manner to their army. In truth I loved the creamy-white flower heads, so useful in pressed flower work, which was one of my hobbies. On one border, which was cleared of all herbaceous plants whilst I painstakingly hand-weeded every piece of ground elder and its root to a trowel depth. Bucket after bucket, barrow after barrow-load of vegetation was consigned to the bonfire. Satisfied at last with the dark earth cleansed of every trace I set about replanting the area. One spit down with the spade and there it was, another matted area of root. It was then that I decided I had to learn to live with it. If I had researched it fully then I would have discovered that I could have cooked with it. If I'd consumed enough I may even have eradicated it!

I undertook a huge campaign of restoration. I would take a piece of shrub up to Arthur who would identify it for me, then send me away to lookup its cultivation and propagation requirements in a book. I didn't use any of Arthur's books instead '*The Readers Digest Gardening Encyclopaedia*' became my bible. Having researched its needs; out into the garden I went to apply the information. This is how I learnt to garden. I found the line drawings for pruning particularly useful. Many of the shrubs were choking with detritus in their centres. A great deal of satisfaction was had, reclaiming these old shrubs and giving them a new lease of life.

Several friends were lost at this time - the ones who objected to having a conversation with my rear. They would arrive well-dressed admitting this was deliberate, so that I couldn't ask them to 'just give me a hand'.

Others would telephone and say with incredulity that they couldn't understand why I was doing what I was doing or how I would manage. A cordless telephone helped during these conversations as I became adept at deadheading and chatting within a one hundred foot radius of the house. The good friends came in gardening clothes with gloves. Taking themselves off to get a bucket, a kneeler and wheelbarrow before joining me for a chat and an hours' work. They were easily satisfied too. A dozen eggs, a cup of tea or a sandwich lunch as 'payment'. Good friends indeed.

I loved all the early work and took over with pride. Now this was my garden to rescue from the neglect. It would be my memorial to Gay. However the entire garden did not become solely mine for a further seventeen years; when I would be able to do anything I liked without the constraints or comments, disagreement and criticism of others. At that point it became a memorial to them both.

When I moved into Orchards the path leading from the kitchen to the outbuildings had disappeared beneath the *Cedrus deodara,* its branches extending across the back border. All that remained of the west lawn was a narrow strip at the front. I removed the lower branches, rediscovered the path and rebuilt the sandstone wall. I appreciated the tree; now for its sheer size, the rugged bark of the trunk, the feathery light green new growth. I loved to look up through its spreading canopy to the specks of sky above. It grew two to three feet a year, the new growth waving like a flag in a breeze. A few years later the shingle roof at the back of the house began to crumble, all light and air blocked by the volume of the cedar's growth. The decision was made to remove this great lady of a tree. 'Fell her piecemeal' was the instruction given to the tree surgeon. Returning from work one afternoon, she had been stripped of her side branches and felled across the sandstone wall and left in huge chunks for me to deal with; but the stump had been left standing three feet high, rugged bark intact.

Not long after the cedar's felling, the hurricane of 1987 raged throughout the night. My youngest daughter Sorcha crept beneath my duvet and squealed every time she saw one of the tall conifers bend almost double. The wind swept a swathe of destruction through the garden, bringing native and ornamental trees down like nine pins. The cedar was within this path and - had it remained - could have fallen and crushed the house.

Many of the trees that were either uprooted by the wind or severely damaged were of no great consequence apart from their age. A specimen *Sequoiadendron giganteum* - the Giant Redwood - lost its top; its columnar shape gone forever. It remained one of my favourite trees - fattening outwards instead of slimming upwards. Still beautiful, with soft spongy fissured bark (often shed and used in Christmas decorations) and a huge girth with half a dozen new leaders. Fortunately Arthur was not a perfectionist and he allowed the tree to live on, if not in its true glory. Arthur on a positive note, now aged eighty-four cleared the area nearest the bungalow and began to plant more trees and rhododendrons, knowing full well that he would never see them reach maturity.

One of my first forays on the twin long borders on the western edge of the front lawn at Orchards found me dealing with a bramble that was so thick at the base it must have been there for years. It scrambled for yards up and through a variegated holly and across other shrubs nearby, layering itself at every opportunity where a stem touched the ground. I dug around, pulled

86

and tugged, dug beneath and heaved again at the thug until I had him out (have you noticed how often the worst weeds are masculine?) roots and all. I laid him out on the grass between the two long borders. He measured seven yards.

I loved all the different aspects of gardening. When I had the energy I loved to tackle a difficult or neglected area, cutting, clearing, inch by inch in some cases, until the swamped shrub was clear of bramble, bindweed or sweet bryony. There was something cathartic about liberating a shrub from its former strangled and entangled state to give it a new chance -a new lease of life.

Losing my Grip

My troubled marriage came to an end in 1983. All the earlier hard work had lapsed and the garden had become very overgrown and neglected once again. My divorce was finalised in 1985. The garden became more unkempt and the house more derelict when I undertook full time employment to support my children. The situation for me became more negative and by 1988 I was forced to put the house on the market. With no fenced or defined boundaries and the same arguments raising their ugly heads; I dug my heels in and withdrew the house from sale. Then in 1989 I met Philip.

Rosemary Verey

Although Arthur showed interest in my initiatives in the garden at Orchards; it was not he who gave me the most encouragement. Instead it was an old family friend, the late Rosemary Verey. I met Rosemary in 1978 during a visit with Arthur to Barnsley House in Gloucester following Gay's death. Rosemary held Gay in high regard, giving her credit for advice given on developing the temple garden at Barnsley. I know that Gay was impressed with her and the garden she had made with her husband David. My friendship with Rosemary grew from then. She reminded me a little of Gay; both had forthright and down-to-earth personalities.

When we met at Chelsea several years later, she had recently lost her husband David. Where others may have taken a back seat, she was in the garden she had designed answering questions and giving advice. That same year; whilst on a visit to Barnsley, where she gave me space to sell my pressed flower pictures, we talked long and hard about the future of the garden at Orchards. Returning from that visit; I gave up my job to concentrate solely on the garden.

Rosemary Verey and Penelope at Chelsea

It was Rosemary who gave me the inspiration to take on the task seriously. I will forever be thankful for her influence on me, her kindness, support, energy and love. In 1990 Rosemary encouraged me to keep a journal. She pointed out that this would instil me with more confidence and make me more aware of what the garden would require. This I did from that day onwards. I had taken notes when visiting shows and other gardens with Arthur leaving with copious lists of 'must haves'. But this journal was of my daily work within the garden and ideas for the different areas. For many years it was only written up from January to March, until garden work overtook me; resumed again from October to the end of December when the lack of daylight drew me indoors. Another sound piece of advice Rosemary gave was, *'to take one idea from wherever you go. Keep it somewhere - in your head, your heart or your notebook - one day it will be used'.*

Do all good gardeners do 'the tour'? Rosemary advised me in the early years to tour the garden every day and take notes, and then I would know exactly what needed to be done. I found this exercise rather depressing. Rosemary's garden was much smaller than mine and she had the luxury of a couple of gardeners. When Philip and I stayed with her for the first time I was impressed by the hard work which she undertook. She rose, breakfasted and was out to meet her gardeners first thing every morning. They walked the garden, she instructed them of the most important jobs for the day. Before they left for home they had to write in a journal all that they had achieved that day. She wrote during the day and into the evening, using candlelight and a green ink fountain pen. Much of her correspondence to me was in green fountain ink too. In 1995 when Philip and I married in Cirencester Registry Office, Rosemary was my 'bridesmaid'; *'the oldest bridesmaid in the world'*, she joked at the wedding breakfast she hosted for us at her home.

With a garden of more than seven acres, not newly made and taken on in such a neglected state, writing a daily journal could be a disheartening task. Moreover, I had no gardeners in the early years - just Philip and myself. Caring for the garden became a way of life; and as I prepared for bed, my head would mull over the options for the following day's work. That said it is sound advice for people with a more manageable size of garden; to go slowly around the garden with a very critical eye and keep notes.

Chapter Two

Labour of Love

What defines 'labour'? The dictionary states, as a noun: physical or mental work; exertion; toil. As a verb: to work hard; exert oneself. A labour of love is a task done for pleasure, not reward. One must assume that the reward indicates monetary incentive; having spent so many years and so much money saving the garden at Orchards; remuneration certainly did not come into it. However the amount of pleasure that the work gave me - despite all the labour - was recompense enough.

The saviours of Orchards were twofold. Meeting Philip in 1989 was the beginning. A saner man would have run a mile or more. Maybe he liked a challenge? Nothing could have proved more challenging than the following fifteen years. On his first visit to Orchards, an ancient double butler sink leant against the dry sandstone wall on the north side of the house; as if to hold back the sandstone that was popping out at awkward angles. What Philip thought I never asked. The hard work was obvious! Signs of neglect were all around. The top long border behind the sandstone wall was full of grass. A solitary *Mahonia* flowered bravely at the edge of the sandstone steps. *Kolkwitzia amabilis* - the Beauty Bush - stood naked in the middle of the long back border, slowly peeling last years' bark. Variegated *Vinca* smothered the wall. *Saxifraga urbinum* - London Pride - dripped in and out of the undulating crevices of sandstone. The crazy-paved area at the top of the steps was awash with weeds and grass. This area became Philip's first project.

North sandstone wall in 1989

Not content with rebuilding the wall, we set to with digger and dumper and removed lorry loads of soil to make a rear paved area. The excavations were taken back as far as the *Kolkwitzia*. The narrow central steps were removed and new; wider curved steps were built. A specimen *Magnolia tripetala* which Gay had grown from a seed - marooned years earlier, its roots cut and then encased in a low brick wall - was freed from its constraints. Topsoil saved from the digging out was laid around it and levelled. The sandstone wall was dismantled stone by stone, set aside for reuse; exposing the yellow clay subsoil. Gradually Philip rebuilt the walls using mortar to hold it together, leaving pockets for planting. The wall to the right of the new steps undulated gently around the corner of the house until it met the narrow sandstone wall that held back the terrace above the east lawn. The late afternoon sun poured in and reflected light back towards the north wall of the house.

Prior to Philip's rebuilding I had removed any worthy plants and potted them up. London Pride had survived happily in the shade and *Campanula poscharskyana* which many considered a weed grew, to my delight, just like one. The few surviving herbaceous plants growing near the *Kolkwitzia* were dug up, cleaned of couch grass and repotted. The grass on the border was killed and the plants reinstated. An *Acer palmatum* 'Dissectum Atropurpureum' bought in 1978 from

Bodnant nursery in Wales was moved to the top of the steps; where in years to come it was to spill across the wall.

This added an entirely new dimension to the north face of the house, brightening and broadening the view from the kitchen windows and offering a wealth of new planting opportunities. The grass at the top of these steps was still very rough and the narrow border in front of the low sandstone wall near the swimming pool was weedy and overgrown. Philip relaid the other low sandstone walls to the east of the house. We lifted *Rosa* 'Excelsa' from the ground and tied it to the new larch pole and rope support that Philip had erected.

His love, support and physical effort allowed my dreams to come true. The other saviour was me. Together we transformed the beautiful woodland garden. Another achievement ran parallel to the garden - the opening of my own specialist nursery.

Moving Forward

Within hours of Arthur's death I found myself, during a telephone interview with Robin Lane Fox, Gardening correspondent for the Financial Times, committing myself to opening the garden to the public. I wanted to share Arthur's garden with the readers of his many books, to give access to the space that gave him inspiration and to carry out a wish that was Gay's dream. I needed to keep their memories alive. It was a decision that surprised neither Philip nor me, even though we had never discussed it. My small nursery, opened the previous autumn and disbanded within a couple of weeks when Arthur became unwell, was to be reopened in the spring. But to open the garden? It seemed like the obvious step to take. Now I concentrated one hundred percent on propagation and preparing the nursery for opening the following March.

After making contact with the National Gardens Scheme, my local area supervisor agreed that we could open the following year. She was to write to me later saying that I had *'exhausted her with my enthusiasm'*. When she arrived the following spring prior to our first open day she was impressed and amazed at the renovation thus far; admitting that she had not thought we could possibly achieve all that I had enthused about. May 1994 was the month chosen for our first opening. The weather was perfect for the entire weekend, azure blue sky and sunshine. The garden glowed. Late frost had browned the *Magnolia* flowers; but the red and yellow tulips from Arthur and Gay's era detracted the eye and lit the borders, while forget-me-nots crowded between the lush growths of the emerging herbaceous plants. Jean Painter, Matron from Red Oaks and a small gang of her less elderly residents, all ex-gardeners, came weeks before to help me pot up stock for sale in the nursery, returning on the open day to help with teas and plant sales. I think I learnt more over those weeks than I had learnt so far.

'Why haven't you cut down the *Fuchsias*?' One of the residents enquired.

'Arthur said to leave them until the new growth broke.'

'Don't wait, cut them in the autumn, make a wigwam with the prunings to protect the crowns from frost and remove them in late spring.' This advice I repeated throughout my gardening days and applied to *Lavatera* x *clementii* 'Barnsley' and *Lavatera thuringiaca* 'Ice Cool'. It gave the winter garden a more orderly appearance and enabled a head start on the busy spring schedule. They liked the way I worked in the greenhouse; approved of my old towel hanging on the hook. Another gentleman gave me an article that Arthur had written in February 1960 about his nursery, claiming that the article had done wonders for his trade.

He said that he could think of no one better to donate the article to.

In return for their kindness I presented Red Oaks with a large oval picture of pressed flowers, all of which had come from the garden at Orchards, set on dark green silk. Matron held a small acceptance tea party at Red Oaks. They had a brass plaque made to be put beneath the picture.

We had a hugely successful opening, coverage on television and in many of the local and county newspapers. We were exhausted and exhilarated at the end of the bank holiday weekend.

**Penelope presenting her pressed flower picture
to Jean Painter - Matron of Red Oaks**

Chapter Three

Shady Ladies

Shade is a useful attribute to any garden. At Orchards the shade and shadow began at sunrise and continued until sunset. It gave a sense of movement, leading the eye from one area to another. The mature trees and shrubs in the garden were in abundance; they cast ever changing patterns as the sun moved across the sky, varying again on the season; transforming the mood and drama of the plantings. Lower; longer shadows in winter and spring. The shadows cast at sunset were in some ways the most glorious. Even after a long, grey day the sun so often revealed itself just before it set; bathing the garden with washes of yellow, orange and bronze hues.

Shade - feared and considered a problem by so many - is as useful an aspect of the garden as any other. In fact if you have no shade in your garden; one small tree could be planted to create a shady area. Shade comes in many forms. Dappled shade sends shafts of sunlight through tree canopies or gaps between trees. This shade allows more light under deciduous trees from autumn until the new spring growth comes.

Part shade; when the sun reaches a place for only part of the day. For example; an east wall - which receives sun for a few hours in the morning - a building, a tall tree or a west wall which will only receives the setting sun. A north wall will get no sunlight at all unless light is bounced off something else - like the sandstone walls at Orchards and also the light reflected from the back patio. So many plants can be grown in the shade, even those given a recommendation for sun. More attention may be needed to ensure their wellbeing. Many require a thick mulch if the ground is dry otherwise they could be prone to disease. Experience taught me to be adventurous, try anyway, but be watchful.

One successful planting in a colleague's garden was directly beneath the raised canopy of a mature oak tree. This border, tucked away in the furthest corner, related to approximately one quarter of the entire garden. Well mulched except near the trunk of the oak, the dark earth was uplifted by the brightness of large plantings of *Rudbeckia* var. *sullivantii* 'Goldsturm', the structural form of *Acanthus spinosus, Hostas* and ferns which brought an otherwise dull corner alive.

In my own garden beneath the canopy of *Prunus* 'Kanzan', *Houttuynia cordata* 'Chameleon', a marginal plant made a wonderful carpet. The border was mulched after a wet period but not very deeply. We never had the time to dig it in; letting the worms do the work for us.

Prunus 'Kanzan' border

Planted in the shade the *Houttynia* may not have grown as tall or flowered as prolifically but after a few years it spread its brightly variegated leaves in hues of green, pale yellow and red, intermingling with *Tellima grandiflora* and *Arisarum proboscideum* - the Mouse Plant. This plant requires humus rich moist soil in part shade. Only one criterion was met; the shade, but it survived well; making a good clump of glossy dark green arrow-shaped leaves. The dark brown-purple spathes are hooded with a long tapering tip, hence its

101

common name. *Glechoma hederacea* - Ground Ivy - was allowed to run through this planting. Although invasive if the soil is too rich, the delightful blue flowers in early spring made it a useful addition. It was then weeded away in late spring. *Geranium macrorrhizum* 'Bevans' made an enormous spread on the other side of the *Prunus* 'Kanzan'. Fortunately it responded well to severe pruning.

We extended this small border down the garden so that the shade at the far end was neither as deep as directly underneath the canopy, nor as dry. Planted here were more surprises. Scarlet flowered *Monarda* 'Squaw' thrived. Attempts to introduce it, in other more sunny borders failed; it succumbed to mildew. Here there was none and it produced copious numbers of flowers. Dark purple-green stems of *Ligularia przewalskii* stood six feet high, bearing dense racemes of yellow flower heads in mid to late summer, above lush deeply cut irregularly lobed palmate leaves. *Phlomis russelliana* created another tall statement and by September the hooded yellow flowers had developed into rusty brown seed heads in whorls along the flowering stem. The leaves on these stems took on a butter-yellow appearance, whilst the woolly basal leaves grew larger, holding the early morning dew. Because of the shade afforded to this area *Lysimachia ciliata* 'Firecracker' flourished. Grown elsewhere, drought speckled their bronzed maroon leaves with grey mildew, leading me to believe that shade was more important than the dryness. *Alchemilla mollis* grew here, but then it grew anywhere; I never tired of such an easy plant.

Epimedium's became a passion (I developed many of those over the years). Arthur had grown two species. One was *E. davidii* a clump-forming evergreen with pale to deep yellow spurred flowers on spikes held above the leaves. The old foliage was trimmed away before the flower spikes formed; revealing the beauty of the coppery new leaves before they turned bright green. The other was a yellow flowered *E grandiflorum* a deciduous species with heart-shaped leaflets bronzed when young. The pendent spurred flowers unfurl at ground level and hold the buds as the reddish stems emerge. One clump caught the late sun in March giving the stems an almost transparent redness. Lying on the path to capture the image was difficult enough without Saffron - our Parsons Jack Russell, affectionately licking my nose.

103

I added several more from the *E. grandiflorum* group; but none did as well as the ones that Arthur had established. To this I added several cultivars from the *E* x *youngianum* species which included 'Niveum' - white-flowered, 'Merlin' - dusky-mauve flowers, the young leaves flushed purple and 'Roseum' which has variable foliage and dusky-pink to purple flowers. I found this species a little more difficult to keep growing strongly. By far the most special; was *E* x *warleyense*; for me an entirely different colour; the sepals reddish-orange, with yellow flowers and mid green leaflets tinted red in spring and autumn which complimented perfectly a newly purchased *Acer palmatum* 'Katsura', with bright orange palmate leaves in spring, mellowing to yellow in summer, changing to both hues in autumn before deepening to pink. *Euphorbia robbiae* could be a nuisance in anything other than dry shade and poor soil. The yellow-green bracts were long-lasting. *Luzula sylvatica* 'Aurea' a favourite grass added a golden highlight to a shady area, with *Ajuga reptans* 'Braun Hertz' which carried candles of blue flowers, its burgundy foliage creeping through the *Luzula's* leaves.

What a joy to walk along the path before Christmas to see the first dark stems of *Helleborus* 'Early Purple' begin to unfurl. I reflected often what was the most interesting, the most inspiring; the early dark stems, the purple buds waiting to unfold, sometimes held still by an early frost, or the *Helleborus* x *hybridus* seedlings, some of the most beautiful shady ladies of early spring; an eclectic mix of diversely coloured and patterned flowers. By late March a few buds were still to open, along with the developing seedpods from early flowers, revealing the shiny black seeds and the prospect of even more seedlings. Even I had been known to spend 'serious' money on hellebores of deep dusky plum-black with a bloom covering the petals. A double creamy-green colour and a green flowered were two of my most unusual, but my own seedlings were the most exciting. We moved these outwards around the garden, making another shady border of them beneath the *Cornus kousa*.

The late Dick Robinson - formerly the owner of Hyde Hall (now a Royal Horticultural Society garden) - walked along the garden path early one year and enquired as to why I had not already removed the old leaves from my hellebores, which if left, lay themselves flat to the ground to make way for the flowers and new foliage. 'Time or lack of it' was my usual answer.

'Make time! The job should be done by Christmas Day; remember that; especially if the leaves are diseased. Once they lay on the soil that too becomes contaminated. If you've nothing better to do on Christmas Day when the lunch is cooking do it then.' I didn't like to tell him that we went to the pub whilst the turkey was cooking! However I did remember his words and from then onwards removed the old leaves well before Christmas. *Helleborus* 'Early Purple' and the oldest hellebore seedlings were beneath the canopy of a silver birch and witch hazel. Their deciduous mulch was further enhanced with mushroom compost in autumn or early spring. Dick and his wife Helen both became good friends and stalwart supporters of our work. Helen visited the garden with her local gardening group. I received a brief note following this visit. Helen declared that our *Euoynmus europaeus* 'Red Cascade' was the best specimen she had ever seen. She congratulated us on our work, and concluded, '*Your father would have been very proud of your efforts.*'

Heuchera, Tellimas and *Tiarellas* are all excellent plants in well mulched shade. The former did not grow very well; vine weevils loved them. Sluggish in the

106

garden they needed more attention than I was able to give them. Two easy shade lovers unknown to many garden visitors were *Maianthemum bifolium* a perennial woodlander for cool spots; similar to a small lily of the valley; sprays of white flowers were followed by red berries. Once established it flourished, spreading by rhizomes and seeds. The other; *Mitella breweri* with racemes of yellowish-green fringed-petaled flowers, from late spring onwards; on stems six inches high above their hairy lobed mid green leaves mingled well with late bright blue flowers of *Brunnera macrophylla* and *Omphalodes cappadocia.*

Striving to make garden maintenance easier we linked the trees and shrubs from Gay and Arthur's time, thus making large borders around several otherwise specimen plantings. It gave a more tidy effect to the garden and made grass cutting easier. The most important job initially was to keep these borders weed free; before planting was introduced. The different types of shade are well defined in an excellent book; *'Shade Plants for Garden & Woodland'* by George E Brown. Reading his book thoroughly made me much less afraid of shade. Observation within your own space is an important rule but many of the other rules can be broken.

Geranium phaeum seedlings in varying hues of amethyst, their gold stamens set against the solid tones flowered for two months or more in the shade of *Magnolia tripetala* outside the kitchen window. Lilac-flowered *Geranium* x *monacense* with its reflected petals added more interest. A further delight were the finches that visited during early flowering, to catch caterpillars and small insects, through to the seeding of the plants, when both finches and mice returned to feed on the seeds.

Cyclamen hederifolium nestled in deep leaf litter beneath an old hawthorn tree. The seeds originally came from the rounded ripe pods which spiralled down and lay on the earth in Arthur's Jersey garden. Years of deciduous mulch made the soil in this area very light and peaty. Ground elder tried its best to take over, but here it was easy to remove the leaves and roots - and gently push back any tiny cyclamen seedlings that may have been disturbed. In later years I planted *Cyclamen coum* nearby for a longer display of flowers.

Enchanter's nightshade - *Circaea lutetiana* - enjoyed the same peaty conditions, spreading its thin white roots just beneath the surface. I left this delicate perennial to its own devices until mildew developed on its leaves, only then cutting it back to ground level or removing any that we didn't want. The tiny deeply notched two-petaled white flowers faded to pink, developing minute oval seedpods covered in hooked thistles. I loved this flower for pressing; the pods green or brown, the tiny stems of both flowers and seedpods making a useful delicate and airy addition to my pressed flower pictures. Depending on its situation the green leaves were sometimes flushed purple. Elephant Hawk Moth caterpillars feed on this species.

The north wall of the house; the brick extension of 1959 remained unadorned until 1978 when I planted *Hedera helix* 'Goldheart' to the side of the wide kitchen window. This was a mistake. One that was left for about twenty years until I felt confident enough to remove it completely. As a young plant I was able to cut out the dark green growth from 'Goldheart', necessary to keep the yellow variegation. As it scrambled ever upwards towards the light and out of easy reach; green foliage took over and all was lost. It wrapped itself across the windows in the blink of an eye; yet it remained still because I loved the flowers and berries in autumn which attracted wasps, bees and birds. Several times it was used by a charm of wrens clustered together for warmth. With new confidence I cut a two foot section from the main stem and left it to die. A few weeks later it was removed, in huge 'trellis-like' sections from the facade without causing any damage to the brickwork. Any new growth from the stem which remained in the narrow border was treated with systemic weedkiller until the ivy gave up its fight for life.

Clematis cirrhosa var. *balearica's* freckled bell-shaped flowers became lost in the lush growth of the ivy and scrambled equally quickly to the apex of the roof where it flowered happily to be viewed only from the top of the steps. A narrow trellis was fixed all around the large picture window, the clematis was tied in neatly; two paving slabs were lifted, the earth removed and replaced with topsoil and grit and *Rosa* 'Kathleen Harrop' - thornless like its parent *R.* 'Zéphirine Drouhin' - with shell-pink fragrant flowers from June well into winter and *R.* 'Zéphirine Drouhin' semi-double cerise-pink flowers over several months, with the added interest of the young shoots and leaves in bronzy hue, were tied into the trellis.

On the other side of the back door an earlier planting

of *Hydrangea petiolaris,* once well established became a nuisance; trained around the wall towards the downstairs bathroom all the shoots seemed to creep directly for the window or push up under the eaves. We tried to keep everything within easy reach of the top of a pair of steps. During the summer months, *Clematis* 'Jackmanii' cascaded green-stamened velvety-purple four-sepalled blooms from the framework of the hydrangea.

Natures' food is the best mulch for shady areas. Large wire containers were added to the wooden compost bins behind the outbuildings. Autumn leaves were raked into piles and collected by hand or in larger areas with the tractor mower. Over the years more wire containers were placed around the garden and filled. No special treatment was ever given to any of the compost making. One year I experimented with leaves in old compost bags; punched with holes to aerate, some had a chemical compost accelerator added, others didn't. There was no difference between the contents of the bags. They all became difficult to handle and the leaves remained whole and slimy. Of the other compost heaps; we had neither the time nor the energy to turn them, except for removing the top layers into the

111

next door bin when you could see the brown crumbly compost below. The bins, not the wire containers as they were too tall, did particularly well whilst we kept our pygmy goat!

Cornus kousa border

One advantage of shade in the garden is the long period of interest in foliage and flower throughout the year. Once the specimen trees were linked together into large borders, the range of shade planting became extensive. Under the *Cornus kousa* - which became very important to me as a photograph of Arthur had been taken in front of it in 1992, for the frontispiece of Country Life Magazine, to celebrate his ninetieth birthday - we added to the pure white hellebore that

Rosemary Verey had given us. We planted more than sixty seedlings of *Helleborus* x *hybridus*, with subtle shades of white flushed with green, pink tinged with green, and deep plum, some spotted, some not.

We planted a seed tray of *Eranthis hyemalis* donated by Rosemary. She would sow entire trays of fresh seed and transplant the newly germinated seedlings intact. This was a plant that Arthur had not managed to introduce into the garden. Hundreds of bulbs of *Galanthus* 'Atkinsii' a taller growing snowdrop than *Galanthus nivalis* were lifted in the green and planted randomly. The double form of *Galanthus nivalis* was grouped nearer the edges, along with *Scilla messeniaca* which naturalised freely when happy, which it was. Rosettes of broad, bright green leaves, nestled beneath spikes of numerous bright blue flowers each held on one centimetre long pedicels. The ripened seeds of this and the *Galanthus* were pulled and scattered at will across the border. A mixture of other plants were added to this border, *Geranium thunbergii*, *G macrorrhizum* varieties, *Silene fimbriata, Dicentra spectablis* 'Alba', *D.* 'Bountiful' and *D. formosa, Geum rivale* 'Album', G. r. *'Leonard's Variety'* along with the elegant willow gentian - *Gentiana asclepiadea* - a

113

late flowering herbaceous perennial with arching stems which carried dark to light blue trumpet flowers.

Many of the *Campanula* family thrive in the shade, the single forms of *C. persicifolia* did well but I struggled to keep the double forms. I had read that *C. glomerata* is a wanderer - I wish that it had wandered in my borders. I managed to keep it from year to year but only just. One of my favourites was the nettle-leaved *Campanula trachelium* var. *alba* and *C.t.* 'Bernice', a lilac-blue double, whose bells stand upwards as if to greet you. I loved the rough texture of its leaves, both the flowers and the leaves offer a complete contrast to *Campanula punctata* with its erect spikes of pendent creamy-white to dusky-pink tubular bell-shaped flowers spotted red and hairy within.

Thalictrum minus, given to me by a garden visitor as a 'must have' plant, became invasive but it was forgiven for its show of buttery-yellow foliage in autumn. The diversity of *Thalictrum* added interest and drama to several of the borders. A particular favourite was *Thalictrum delavayi* 'Album', the long yellowish-white stamens extended far beyond the pure white bracts like streamers blowing in a breeze.

The taller the trees and shrubs grew, the more shade

of one kind or another they afforded. Many of the plants chosen or allowed to seed would have been regarded as a nuisance in other peoples' gardens, or, for the more discerning gardener, considered inferior. However I loved natures' way of increasing my ground cover with very little effort from me, save the scattering of a seedpod or two. Quite often it would be the wildlife that would do the spreading for me.

One clump of yellow Welsh poppies thrived under the *Magnolia tripetala* behind the house; the only direct sunlight they enjoyed was a brief moment as the sun was on its way down behind the trees. One evening, we watched a mouse making his way along a delicate seeding stem which bowed over the sandstone wall towards the paving slabs. The mouse clung on until it slid unceremoniously to the ground. It scampered towards the steps and moments later the undergrowth could be seen moving; within seconds he was back to try again. I introduced *Scutellaria altissima* to the garden; so enamoured was I by its erect habit, the nettle-like leaves and spikes of pretty two-lipped flowers, the upper erect and blue, the lower lip white and the skull-cap shaped seed heads, that I encouraged it to colonise around the garden.

The lower east lawn proved to be an untidy patch. Arthur's concrete paths had lasted well. As a child I remember a narrow strip of grass which had edged a low sandstone wall, with a wide herbaceous border between it and the path.

East herbaceous border - 1950s

Leading up to his retirement Arthur did away with many of the herbaceous borders, planting shrubs in some and grassing others over. The east herbaceous border - pictured above - was laid to lawn, leaving the narrow border beneath the low sandstone wall with a few herbaceous plants and bulbs. Time for a change! Philip widened the existing border, cut three widths with the lawn mower, and then removed the remaining grass. The soil was turned and composted leaving me with two equally wide borders. The growth of the shrubs on the south side cast light open shade. I had fallen in love with *Salix integra* 'Hakuro-nishiki', its mottled white and pale pink foliage irregularly blotched and patchy. I bought twelve half-standard trees each grafted on to a straight stem of another willow. They travelled home stuffed in the back of my Nissan Prairie, along with a colleague in the front seat, who had to endure their twiggy growth poking in her ears! The stems of 'Hukuro-nishiki' were rather weak and lax, exposing coral red stems in autumn when the foliage had fallen. Six were planted opposite each other in the two borders. The spring and summer foliage illuminated the newly named Salix Walk, the grafted canopies resembled sparklers. They didn't survive for many years; I think the exuberance of my underplanting proved too much competition for the little trees, plus the shade from the front border became deeper as those shrubs matured. After they were removed *Nectaroscordum siculum* subsp. *bulgaricum* gave height to the borders; though not on the same scale. This was one of my favourite plants with multiple interest, from the pointed, papery calyx in which were

117

encased lots of flower buds held high above the twisted leaves. As the swelling buds pushed open the calyx they dropped down, opening their pendent bell-shaped thimble-sized cream flowers. They were marked with burgundy and flushed green at the base on the outside, a deeper shade on the inside. When flowering ended the seed heads pointed themselves upwards again.

Another passion was the more unusual *Digitalis* species. The native foxglove was encouraged to seed. We moved any seedlings together in groups to make more impact, especially near old stumps or fallen trees. *Digitalis ferruginea, D. parviflora* and *D. lutea* did better with us than *D x mertonensis* - I loved this dusky pink foxglove but it barely lasted a season. *Digitalis ferruginea* gave height to the same border with tall stems of an unusual shade of pale golden brown flowers. *Allium cristophii* was planted in groups of three at intervals along the borders; these too looked like fireworks exploding. Taller statements were made with *Allium* 'Purple Sensation' with rich violet-purple flowers.

Aquilegia species and cultivars were another obsession, the new introductions from Plant World Seeds in Devon, gave added enchantment - *Aquilegia*

'Mellow Yellow' a gold leaved form glowed in the shade, almost all its seedlings came true, its white or milky-blue flowers complimented the foliage perfectly. I purchased numerous different *Aquilegia* seeds, for the most part, they misbehaved delightfully. One year with a cleared area at the top of the twin long borders I scattered mixed *Aquilegia* seed saved from many of the plants in the garden. I was rewarded with an arc of different plants of varying heights, single and double flowers, long spurred, spurless and every tone of colour in the white, pink, blue, cream, yellow and black spectrum. It was a charming spectacle which lasted a couple of years until a decision was made on the permanent planting in this area. A form of toad lily - *Tricyrtis* 'White Towers' - gave late flowers, its leaves turning a dark chestnut brown, which glistened with frost in early winter.

Nature infiltrated at will. We never described our grass as lawn, wild flowers were evident in every area, nestling down, flowering on shorter stems in the freshly mown grass. In the wilder parts of the garden *Claytonia sibirica* carpeted the ground beneath the mature shrubs and trees, it didn't mind what situation it grew in, although the growth and the number of pink

119

flowers would be variable. These areas were left uncut until late summer to allow further seeding. It became one of the most popular woodlanders for sale in the nursery. *Claytonia* leaves can be eaten either raw or cooked. The leaves are bland with an earthy aftertaste similar to raw beetroot. The corrugated sheeting atop an old wooden shed played host to a 'roof' of claytonia, long before 'living roofs' became popular.

Arthur had encouraged bluebells into the bottom south-west woodland of black alder, silver birch, hazel and spindly self-sown oak trees. *Oxalis acetosella* - Wood Sorrel - with snow-white flowers and bright green leaves followed the bluebells. Adjacent to this copse, where further native and planted conifer specimens gave a very shady location *Chrysosplenium* - Golden Saxifrage - ran through the woodland floor where the grass no longer grew. *Geranium robertianum,* dock and stinging nettles covered the denser shade; an important wildlife habitat for butterfly and moth eggs and larvae. Nearby flourished a spread of lily of the valley enjoying the dry peaty soil; planted by Gay in the early thirties.

Dactylorhiza fuchsii - the Common Spotted Orchid - introduced itself in the late 1970s beneath the canopy of

Catalpa bignonioides 'Aurea'. This colony increased substantially over the years, carefully managed by Philip and me. With the grassy area beneath the *catalpa* left to grow, the orchids seeded freely. We mowed in towards the trunk of the mature tree hoping to contain the seeds within this area. Seventy escapee seedlings were transplanted to under the remaining mature apple tree in the bottom orchard. Plugs of plant and soil were dug with the bulb planter to ensure that the orchids would grow on in the soil they liked. Lady Sudeley - a dual-purpose apple tree - had a short trunk and wide spreading branches, its large red-green apples with cream flesh were ripe in September. The meadow that we developed under the tree was enlarged taking in the naturalised daffodils in the lower garden, this area was cut after the daffodil leaves had died back and a circle was cut around the outside of the tree's canopy. This area was lush with wild flowers, some moved from other areas of the garden, others grown from seed or bought as bulbs; *Primula veris, Prunella vulgaris, Leucanthemum vulgare* - Ox-eye daisies and *Centaurea nigra* - Common Knapweed, bird's-foot trefoil, white and red clover, buttercups, sorrel with rusty-red flower stems, plantain with its creamy white ruff circling the

121

brown flower were added to the native grasses, stitchwort and tall thistles which grew there already, developing flowers now the grass was left long. I planted hundreds of *Fritillaria meleagris* one autumn only to have the majority of them eaten the following spring by the rabbits. The meadow was cut down before the apples had ripened, the hay dried and stored for our pygmy goats.

Several dark corners of the garden were lit by small colonies of *Cardamine bulbifer and C. pratensis* where they were allowed to flourish. Speedwell ran a blue river through the grass in many places looking prettiest flowing beneath the apple trees. The bright reddish-purple flowers of *Stachys officinalis* escaped from the Herb Garden and settled in the longer grass in the wild garden on the northern edge. Free passage was given to the variegated form of *Lamium galeobdolon* within the west shelter belt, contained in late summer with either a small lawn mower or a brush cutter. Once I made the mistake of introducing it to a shady border where after an annual mulch, it was up and away, smothering all its neighbours. The purple-leaved form of *Ajuga reptans* ran through the grass making interesting patterns - we left it to run. Bluebells flowered less prolifically in the deeper shade of three mature hornbeams; the scant blueness lit up by the greater stitchwort; an untidy perennial carrying lax clusters of starry white flowers, and tufts of perennial grasses.

The Bluebird henhouse

Shade also has an effect on animals. Whilst I would be collecting together my garden tools after a day's work, my hens would have already gone to bed. Many people have said that hens are stupid but they're not. They have an intelligence of their own that others do not understand. The sun dipped behind the shelter belt long before it set. My hens read the signs and settled for the night. The native birds gathered later, chattering about their day before they too roosted. If we were late coming to put them away, the hens would have already taken themselves into their 'house'; from the large outer daily run to the smaller inner area and up the 'ladder' that Philip built, into their very own caravan aptly named 'Bluebird'.

A retaining wall (built by Arthur from left over breeze blocks - which crumbled and slipped towards the level below) ran along the edge of the nearby lawn. *Symphytum* 'Hidcote Pink' had naturalised, its roots binding the soil, along and down towards the chicken run. I made no move to curb its spread. In a garden of seven plus acres I welcomed the colonies of self-seeding plants. At one time it had been our intention to clear the area and build steps down from this lawn. This idea was lost in the mistiness of too much other work. On a narrow arid border which ran along the south-facing wall of the outbuildings, where several ivies and jasmine struggled to grow, hybridised *Symphytum* marched itself along like an invading army.

A small group of knowledgeable garden visitors sat with me one morning on the lawn in front of the outbuilding, drinking tea after a guided walk around the garden. 'One of your problems,' a colleague had told me, 'is that you have no shame.' She was referring to the fact that I was quite prepared to admit when I didn't know the answer to a question about the garden or a plant. At this moment I did feel shame and great discomfort sitting in such close proximity to what a lot of people considered to be very undesirable weeds. But I loved hogweed; their height, their structure, their creamy-white umbels and I was amazed at the number of small insects that had an affinity with the plant; tiny hoverfly, honeybees, wasps, and red soldier beetles to name just a few. I was glancing at these statuesque stems.

'Do you like them; was it your intention to leave them?' One lady asked me.

'I do and I did,' I replied. 'It drives some people wild but I love them.' I continued as if to justify myself, 'But I always cut them down before they seed.' The group had all turned to admire the stems. Everyone agreed that although some of them didn't have the space to leave such plants in their gardens, they would, if they had enough room, do so. My kind of gardeners.

The mallow was another plant I didn't wage war against. It particularly liked the *Rosa rugosa* hedge and the Herb Garden where by mid-summer it would be covered in rust. Only then did I cut it to ground level and within days was rewarded with fresh leaves.

All this wildness was pleasing to my eye. Nothing too contrived; carpets of self-sown forget-me-nots brightened all the yellowness of spring. Most delightful were the lichen species on the sandstone walls and on many of the apple trees in shades of lime and greyish-green as well as moss on steps and old terracotta pots. One area of the garden had a covering of sphagnum moss which the birds would take for nest making; another had little mounds of closely laid moss; fairy houses I used to tell the children. I accepted misshapen trees and shrubs; roses that extended wayward branches, only tying-in stems that might be caught up or flicked in the face. And even my tying-in was rudimentary, large arches of stems left, rather than horizontals tied to within one inch of their lives.

Chapter Four

Throughout the Year

It didn't really matter where you started the year in the garden at Orchards, because it was never 'put to bed' as so many garden magazines recommend. It was much too large. One day merged into the next at an alarming pace. The work was there in one form or another; bad weather never being an excuse not to do something towards the nursery or the garden, as at that point much could be done in the outbuildings or in the greenhouses. There were jobs to be done in the office too, where indexing new plants, preparing the new nursery catalogue or leaflets for the garden and the bed and breakfast that we offered; writing press releases for the coming season, working on illustrated talks and garden groups often became delayed - the view from the office window too beautiful for me to concentrate. There was no time to daydream but when dark clouds gathered dense steel-grey behind the trees clothed in their late autumn colours of red, gold, brown and purple: then strongly and fleetingly the sun would shine through as it set and the garden would be bathed in gold. The contrast so stark but so striking, then it was gone, leaving me to reflect on what a magical place Orchards was.

My only release from the garden was a fortnight before Christmas; and much of that was taken up with wreath-making for the local farm shop or friends and relations. This was work I enjoyed; there was such a wealth of foliage to be taken from the garden. The back patio was filled with branches cut from golden, red (from *Cryptomeria japonica* Elegans Group) and green conifer, variegated and green holly; stems of rose hips, holly berries and *Viburnum tinus* flower heads made up of tight pink buds, white flowers and black berries depending on their stage of development. Variegated and green leaved box; trails of ivy cut from the woodland some with heads of green flower or black berries. Variegated ivy both large and small leaved. Cones of different shapes and sizes gathered from the garden; some sprayed gold, wired together in threes or fives dependent on their size.

The selection made was wheeled by the barrow load into the kitchen where I could work in the warmth. The scent of warm wet conifer and evergreen shrubs filled the kitchen. A further empty barrow stood behind the full one and any unwanted debris was tossed in that direction. The prepared wreaths and table decorations were then placed outside in the elements waiting for delivery. Any leftover greenery remained on the patio until Christmas Eve when trails of ivy and variegated holly were placed over picture frames and across the long mantelpiece in the lounge, the warmth of the fire drawing out the heady fragrance throughout the festive season.

Once the garden was open to the public it became a tradition for us to work in the garden on New Year's Day. One year with the frost on the ground we collected winter debris and made a bonfire. Another year with milder weather it could be a little weeding - shepherd's purse in particular would overwinter, flowering and seeding in unison throughout the year; *cleavers,* or stickywilly as we called it, was another little devil to be weeded out in January. Or it could be noting the flowers already on their way. After one particularly wet, mild December it was *Geranium pyrenaicum* 'Bill Wallis' which was already covered with bluish-purple flowers. *Acanthus mollis* held eighteen to twenty-four inch long fresh green leaves with the rotted old leaf stalks laying on the soil and their architectural seed heads standing four feet tall.

New growth was emerging just below the previous years' slimy *Hemerocallis* leaves. Cerise flowers of *Cyclamen coum* nestled within crinkled brown decomposing leaves of *Acer palmatum* f. *atropurpureum* var. *dissectum*. For me it could be any job that set my mind back to work; be it the garden, propagation for the nursery and preparation for sales or garden groups and visitors.

Sometimes the tradition of gardening on 1 January would include a walk around the garden and taking notes. Only once did I make a list of *'Jobs to be Done'* the length of it was far too long and much too depressing. Was it A T Johnson who said, *'You must always have a plan even if it's in your head'*? That is where it was for me. Philip and I did sit down occasionally and draw plans on pieces of paper; he was a capable draughtsman so they could have been more professionally drawn up, but I had a problem transferring that information from my mind to the ground. The plot of land at Orchards was not uniform anyway. His eye was as good a guide as any and on hard landscaping we rarely disagreed.

Autumn considered by many a dreary season; it saddens my daughter Sorcha, *'All that death'* she would

130

remark mournfully. For us it came as a relief from all those long days of hard work. The shortening evenings drew you inside, the warmth of the log fire tempting you to sit and watch the flames flicker, until very quickly you would doze before it.

As an outdoor person, working with my hands in the soil, I enjoyed autumn and winter. The expectation of the next season already apparent. Nature's cloak of fallen leaves gave shelter from frosts, to winter and early spring bulbs; adding structure and nurture to the soil. We left the borders covered with leaves. Many visitors had remarked that this encouraged slugs and snails - maybe it did but our birds dealt with the majority of these. We kept the paths clear of leaves and weather permitting the ones on the grass would be gathered by Philip on the tractor and placed in wire containers. Others nearby the shady areas were raked back as natural mulch. *Magnolia* leaves and pine needles were burnt. They took much too long to compost, even when chopped by the lawn mower. The largest leaves of *Magnolia tripetala* could be up to twenty-one inches long; these had to be picked up by hand from beneath the tree and from the path.

The leaves on the deciduous trees began to change colour at the beginning of September, depending on the variety of tree and the weather. Many leaves hung on the trees for an age until a wind snapped off entire ends. There was a gentle dropping of leaves over several weeks; which Philip would find disheartening, but for me, I was thankful that they didn't all descend in one day. Continuous raking and collecting began from the first leaf drop. *Magnolia* x *soulangeana* leaves were collected on the western side of the garden where they blanketed the ground; they were neither moved by the wind nor dried by the sun. In fact, if left the ground became glaciered in colder months. Beneath its canopy the leaves decomposed over time into pretty skeletonised forms.

Many people admired our beech hedge -so did I in its glossy purple foliage - but I didn't like its winter coat. I wished the brown crispy leaves would fall. They rattled like old bones in the wind. It was only when the new buds swelled the following spring that they pushed these old leaves away. Mature beech trees shed their leaves differently depending on their place in the garden. In more sheltered areas the previous year's leaves may remain longer.

The *Liquidambar* in the lower arboretum was tipped deepest mahogany, whilst its lower leaves in more shelter, only managed a scarlet or yellow hue; it resembled an enormous bonfire. Some friends said it reminded them of a volcano; some a beacon, but we all agreed that no description would do it full justice, such was its beauty. The leaves that fell lay beneath the canopy like a rich Persian carpet. A different species of *Liquidambar* on the east of the garden sheltered to the west by an *Arbutus,* remained green in December, turning bright scarlet in late January and February and was almost evergreen, only losing the previous year's leaves as the new ones appeared. *Fraxinus angustifolia* 'Rayswood' turned its feathery foliage maroon or rust and could shed all on a windy night. The three mature hornbeams at the top of the garden, (Gay's favourite trees), had grown into each other with age; their leaf drop was quite sudden, carpeting the ground with buttery-yellow leaves. Saffron would move excitedly with her nose down beneath the pile, sniffing out some interesting scent.

The swamp cypress - *Taxodium distichum* - is one of the few deciduous conifers. An outstandingly beautiful tree and most appropriate for wet soils, it turned a dark rusty-brown - giving an appearance of demise - refreshed again in the spring with light green foliage. Glossy purple berries of *Callicarpa bodinieri* var. *giraldii* 'Profusion' remained intact; the clusters ignored by the birds. A single turquoise-blue fruit nestled within each maroon calyx on *Clerodendrum trichotomum* var. *fargesii*. Why and how could a plant with such foetid foliage, carry such sweetly fragrant flowers to be followed by a truly unique berry colour? The wind, blowing through the large leaves of *Quercus rubra* and *Magnolia tripetala,* sounded like a gentle, steady rainfall. *Acer griseum* foliage warmed to a bright scarlet before leaf fall. Cinnamon bark peeled giving texture and interest.

Fair weather gardeners may miss the subtleties of colour, texture and new buds forming. Thanks to Gay's teachings and my passion for what I was doing, no matter what time of the year, my eyes and senses were constantly open and alert whilst I worked at Orchards. As the herbaceous plants were cutback, rich brown compost was laid on the cleared borders. Dew laden spiders' webs glistened in the early morning sun. Minute diamonds dripped from open panicles of *Panicum* and *Miscanthus.* Fluffy inflorescences' of

Miscanthus now faded from the rich reddish-purple of the unfolding flowers which matured to a silvery hue then white to light beige; closed tightly in the dampness reverting to a dull corn tint. The open panicles of *Panicum* swayed gently in the wind, tiny rubies dripped from their stems. Heart-shaped spikelets of *Brizia media* dangled in open panicles from wire-thin stems; the slightest breeze animated them. The finely margined linear leaves changed to raw sienna from the pale green of spring.

Clouds of birds returned to the garden in autumn. Thirty or more greenfinches landed and uplifted together along the *Rosa rugosa* hedge; fat orangey-red and orange hips ripped open to reveal the darker flesh. These fruits were enjoyed by a variety of birds. The fallen apples in the orchard were feasted on by fieldfares swooping in huge flocks that departed in the same manner. The first time I saw these migratory birds was a few years earlier when they touched down in a large unnamed deciduous *Berberis,* whose pinkish-red berries were still hanging in clusters. They stayed long enough for us to view them through the binoculars and for Philip to correctly identify a bird he hadn't seen since he was a boy. The fallen apples were also

135

browsed by the visiting deer and pheasant. The tits shared the caterpillars and insects still to be found and the woodpecker was back on the hopper several times a day. Pigeons covered the front vista, pecking out grubs and insects. Although they stripped the herbaceous foliage as well, they were welcome for their foraging of the grubs.

In January several different shrubby honeysuckles; *Lonicera fragrantissima, L. standishii, L. syringantha,* along with the Christmas Box; *Sarococca hookeriana, S. h.* var. *humilis* and the winter flowering *Viburnum* x *bodnantense* and *V. farreri* filled the winter garden with fragrance. *Hamamelis mollis* spread wide its aged branches, strange twisted yellow petals filled the air with sweet scent.

Whilst the exuberance of summer was incomparable at Orchards, and the burnished colours of autumn dramatic, winter was in no way a cause for disappointment. *'There is no need for any garden to lack flowers in winter'* - the first sentence of Arthur's article 'Winter Flowers' in *'By Pen and Spade'* edited by David Wheeler - is proof of this belief. This piece elucidates many of the shrubs that were key to the garden in the 1980s; most of which were mature at the time of his writing. It was the late Rosemary Verey who stayed with us one February and declared the garden '*a triumph*': the winter bareness didn't detract her expert eye from the good structure of the mature trees nor from the wealth of beauty soon to come.

Near naked herbaceous borders allowed views across the garden so different to the luxuriance of summer, when any semblance of order was lost. Behind the house the *Juniperus x pfitzeriana* hedge and the heather and conifer border blocked the view throughout the year but behind the latter there was a view through the *Cornus kousa* on into the small arboretum at the top of the garden and - heaven forbid - all the neighbouring houses. We were never invited to view our garden from any of their upstairs rooms and I often felt inquisitive. The intense herbaceous growth accelerated in February and March, semi-evergreen leaves; depending on the mildness of the previous winter, and new foliage in a myriad of colours; brownish-red, pinky-red, yellow, lime green, sometimes with flowers nestling within.

By February, the snowdrops would have pushed their way through the deep mulch of mushroom compost, sometimes in milder winters they were showing by

January. Arthur had planted *Galanthus* 'Atkinsii', a large and robust form, ideal for drift planting; these were followed by *Galanthus nivalis* f. *pleniflorus*, a shorter but lovely double form. Later still *G. ikariae* with its handsome bright green leaves, *Pulmonaria rubra* and *Helleborus* x *hybridus* seedlings and an occasional *Iris unguicularis* bloomed. The buds of which could begin as early as November. It was often a battle between me noticing the tight bud snuggled well down inside the leaves or the slightly taller unfurling bud already nibbled by slugs and snails. Another early favourite was the Plum Tart *Iris*, *I.graminea*, which emitted a fruity fragrance from the purple-lilac flowers, the falls tipped with purple-stripes which nestled deep within its long green leaves. I cut back the foliage of both so they could be more easily admired.

Crocuses opened wide their petals to the first warmth of the sun and the early bees took advantage. There were only a few of the large flowered yellow and purple varieties left in the garden from Arthur's day. In his article 'Winter Flowers' Arthur recommends *Crocus tommasinianus* and yet, to my knowledge, he never grew it. We did, as well as its cultivars; 'Whitewall Purple' and 'Taplow Ruby', all of them thrived in the cleared areas around the trees which were not too overcrowded with other herbaceous plants. In other borders we introduced many more species and cultivars. People complain about the birds pecking off the flowers, we were not as lucky, as either the mice had eaten the corms or the squirrels had dug them up, before growth began. For some reason *Crocus tommasinianus* and its cultivars remained intact and multiplied.

By the end of February the first wild daffodils were out, flowers that were there when Gay and Arthur first saw the land. More hellebore flowers were still to come; fat green snowdrop seedpods developed behind the faded flowers. *Scilla messeniaca* glistened like tiny blue jewels beneath *Magnolia tripetala*. I introduced this tiny bulb from elsewhere in the garden so it could be enjoyed whilst working in the kitchen. Bright green foliage with flower spikes erupting from within the centre, pushing through stray decaying *magnolia* leaves from the previous autumn, a rash of tiny blue bells hung from the bright green stems. Two cherries flowered early. Their habits very different possibly because of their placement but their flowers almost identical. Tight deep pink buds followed by single mid-pink blossoms. *Oemleria cerasiformis* was given to me in the early 1990s by an elderly gardener who lived in a nearby village. After walking around Orchards on a private visit he declared it a 'must have'. He dug me a clump from his garden, delivering it the next day; took my spade and selected the place for it to go. For many it is a boring shrub; definitely not showy. It had a subtleness I loved. Described as making a thicket; with me it did not; it quietly ambled about on a newly formed border in a fairly damp area with poor soil. Pendent racemes of almond-scented white flowers hung within the newly emerging foliage in spring. It became a firm favourite.

Scores of *Camellias* and *Rhododendrons* peppered the more shady borders and drifted through the woodlands. The majority of these had been planted in the early years by Arthur and Gay and some of the *Camellias* had, by the time I took over the garden, grown into small trees. Many remained unnamed. One or two would begin to flower by Christmas; the others would give a long season well into June with all the different forms and colours. Gay had a passion for the small-flowered evergreen *Azalea* with violet-blue or purple flowers like 'Blue Diamond. My favourite was *Azalea mollis* with either yellow or orange sweetly scented flowers in spring followed by brilliant yellow and orange autumn colour.

At the end of March the buds on *Clematis montana* 'Elizabeth' hung like pale pink pearls against the grey hues of the cedar walls of the house; keenness of the eye knew the beauty of what was to come. During the following few days your gaze would be drawn each time to the developing buds and the first pink flowers; once out, your observation turned elsewhere to other emerging flowers; only the vanilla scent halted your footsteps as you walked nearby the archway, forcing you again to look up and smile in appreciation.

Clematis armandii had grown on the west elevation of the house since I was a child. It never thrived and had few flowers. I planted the cultivar *C.a* 'Snowdrift' outside the south facing guest room window. It flowered prolifically; fragrance from the pure white flowers filled the spring air. The buds on the native oaks on the last day of March were often fat and fit to burst. The mature oak behind the cabin, nearby the selling nursery, played host to a blackbird who would sit as high as he could in the evening sunlight and sing

141

his beautiful song. Thrushes used the tall cherries to compete in an evening serenade.

There were only a couple of dozen of the red and yellow tulips that had been in the garden since I was a child; I believed these to be 'Apeldoorn' and 'Golden Apeldoorn', so we added more. We also planted several hundred other tulips in the early years, introducing different shades of red, yellow and purple. Once we began to plant themed borders - 'China Pink' and 'White Triumphator' both lily-flowered forms were added to the pink and white border; 'Spring Green' from the viridiflora group for under the *Magnolia tripetala*; the feathered green on the ivory-white flowers complimented perfectly the verdant mounds of hardy *Geranium* cultivars.

The Peter Nyssen catalogue which arrived in spring and autumn were devoured with delicious anticipation; often bereft of pretty pictures the tantalising descriptions painted a picture in my mind. The only cross-reference was for their cultivation requirements. The prices seemed so inexpensive and probably would have been, if the mice and squirrels had left them to grow; or the rabbits and deer left them to develop flower and seed. The lack of seed irritated me the most.

How could the new additions naturalise, when nature's way was snatched from you, often before the flower had developed?

The rush of spring was lost in the sumptuousness of summer - so much happened in the interim months that it would take a whole new book to describe the colourful borders. I cherished its wildness. My garden was allowed the freedom to flourish naturally which many people admired; I was told many times that Orchards was exactly what a garden should be; but on the other hand I could be very ruthless in controlling it. Cutting back herbaceous growth before the books recommended time; encouraging new growth later in the year. Pruning shrubs and climbers when time allowed. Leaving seed heads - not so much for the birds - but for the seeds which would be collected and sold in the nursery. More than once, I was criticised by a 'colleague', for composting the borders too early, tidying plants or pruning shrubs too soon. Yet later one year she complained about having missed her 'window of opportunity'. 'Loosen up,' I said to myself. I felt that nature and the season should be my guide. All writings on the 'rules' of gardening should be seen as recommendations. Following them to the letter was never a viable option for me.

It was Rosemary Verey who encouraged this 'looseness' in my attitudes. One November, on a visit to Barnsley House I queried her pruning a *Clematis* on the wall of the house. 'Do it now, when you have the time. Have a bucket of compost with you and a can of water. Cutback, water, mulch generously and water again. The plant will respond well.' So the great lady of gardening knew to break with conformity too. She wrote and acted from her own personal experience of gardening.

My favourite conifer was *Cryptomeria japonica* Elegans Group; a reddish dark green colour for most of the year, the tone deepens in intensity to rich mahogany hues throughout autumn and winter. I had thought this was due to the cold, but milder winters showed that this was not what initiated the change; maybe it was the shortening days. Whatever the reason, the contrast between the *Cryptomeria* and the huge unnamed pampas in late autumn and winter was breathtaking. The added joy of this tree was the number of years it had given me pleasure.

The small *Cryptomeria* is to Arthur's left

The old black and white photograph above shows Arthur mowing near this tree as a small specimen. Several decades later, as mature branches swept the grass and layered naturally it made itself into a little colony of delicate foliage of varying heights and shades of green and red; depending on how much light each section received.

The enchantment in the morning when the spires were shrouded with morning dew; or raindrops that clung long after the rain had ceased; tiny diamonds of water glinting in the diluted sun of winter will remain in my memory forever. And the bittersweet delight when one year close to Christmas, strong winds took out the top of one of the taller trees in this colony. We trimmed the jagged tear of the tree and stripped off the lower foliage of the fallen branch. It made a very unusual coloured Christmas tree; the fragrance of the warmed conifer gave extra joy over Christmas.

The *Cryptomeria* colony

Despite the bad press that conifers receive; understandable if you could have seen the height that some of the fifty year old specimens had attained; the beauty of them had been overlooked by me for several years. Many of them also took on a different hue in the colder months. Depending on the variety of tree, new spring growth was greyish-green, bright green, brownish or red. The flowers were red or blue, and their newly forming fruits a soft shade of grey, bright light blue, red or yellow, which matured into tiny little brown cones. When time permitted I would wire these together to make little bunches for Christmas decorations.

Three *Juniperus* x *pfitzeriana* planted behind the house as individual specimens in the early 1950s to block out the view of the new bungalow became increasingly invasive. The spreading branches encroached across the top lawn. These were cut back severely in the early 1990s and the rule 'never cut back into old wood' was broken. The thick stumpy ends looked ugly and upset Philip for quite some time. However, several years later these junipers developed into an interesting structural hedge. New growth flourished along the stumps The sides were clipped annually; the new growth greyish-green against the billowing structured mid green branches above; which in spring were tipped gold with the tapering new growth.

Two more *Juniperus* x *pfitzeriana* were planted halfway down the front vista on either side in the late 1950s. These spread in a similar manner. Since his first visit to Rosemary Verey's garden, Philip had been fascinated by the form and structure of the trees used at

Barnsley. There a less mature *Juniperus* x *pfitzeriana* had had all its lower branches removed. Each spring the new growth was clipped making a neat tabletop. The shade beneath its canopy was an ideal spot for *Helleborus* x *hybridus*, violets, Dutch *Iris*, *Santolina pinnata* subsp. *neapolitana*, *Aquilegias* and *Stachys byzantina*.

We returned from Rosemary's funeral, deep in thought and reflection. It was a beautiful day in every sense. The tiny church in the village of Barnsley was packed. Rosemary's eldest son Charles had extended an invitation to us. Many well known garden designers and photographers were there; they were her friends as well as her colleagues. HRH The Prince of Wales was also present. Refreshments were served in Rosemary's beautiful garden. I was so moved by the presence of the Prince that I wrote to him. I knew that Rosemary had designed and helped to plant the cottage garden at his garden at Highgrove. I explained my connection to Rosemary and told him that I had introduced a hardy *Geranium* after Rosemary and offered him plants of that and another *G. sanguinium* 'Barnsley'. My postman Bernie was bursting with pride when an official envelope was delivered to me with a reply from the Prince. He was even more excited when a few months later I received a second letter thanking me for the *Geraniums* I had sent. The Prince wrote '*I am enormously grateful to you for so generously thinking of sending me those lovely Geraniums for my garden. They arrived safely and have been planted in a suitable spot in the Cottage Garden. I am thrilled with them and cannot thank you enough for such a kind thought. This comes with my warmest best wishes. Yours most sincerely Charles.*'

With Rosemary in mind, Philip removed the lower spreading branches of the junipers which dragged on the grass, making it impossible for one person to cut under them. It was a two-man job; one to hold up the branches, and the other to carefully push the mower beneath. It was also a favourite place for the rabbits to play and hide; near to the abundant herbaceous planting around *Prunus* 'Kanzan'. The juniper foliage would brown and whole branches would die back. With the canopies raised from the ground, the large trunks revealed a more interesting shape, with room to plant. *Cyclamen coum* and *C. hederifolium, Brimeura amethystina* a delicate bulbous perennial with basal, linear green leaves, the pendent pale to dark blue

149

flowers held on slender stalks up to eight inches high; we also grew the white-flowered form, along with *Mitella breweri, Scilla messeniaca* and *Galanthus nivalis* f. *pleniflorus* 'Flore Pleno' soon carpeted the naked soil.

The evergreen trees and shrubs were the constant in the garden; their greenness a neutral backdrop, which gave an atmosphere of calmness; of oneness - a monochrome of green. The spectrum of green tones and hues was immense, added to that, bronze new growth, pinkish tinges, cinnamon, ochre, lime and shrimp-pink. The different foliage shapes were interesting but so were the rainbow of colour and textures of the buds - furry, spiny, soft, sticky, and velvety. I was often overwhelmed by how much nature had to offer. Occasional flowers would go unseen unless the fragrance halted your passage. *Elaeagnus pungens* was one that held its minute creamy-white flowers hidden beneath evergreen glaucous leaves, then the sweetness of their scent would flare your nostrils making you raise the foliage to see tiny insignificant, modest blooms bursting with heady scent It was enough to lift your spirits and make them soar.

Chapter Five

Hedges, Structures, Seats and Statues

Hedges

For many, hedges mark the boundary to their property. Others may be introduced within the garden for a formal layout; or to screen one area from another. As the garden at Orchards developed the need for boundaries became apparent. With the mammoth task of maintaining the garden we developed the land surrounding the house into a more structured and orderly area. The woodland was left as that, but with woodchip paths laid for woodland walks. The specimen trees had been enclosed into long drifting borders. Many of the daffodils on the front vista were moved to within these areas where they could die more tidily.

Arthur and Gay had planted a *Rosa rugosa* hedge that edged the east boundary of the garden along the farm lane. It was both practical and stunning in all its aspects. Untidy, having a bushy habit with attractive compound green foliage made up of five to nine leaflets, the wrinkled surface of which lends itself to the term rugose. The large floppy petals emitted a delicious sweet fragrance which filled the air in summer. The unkempt appearance of the hedge was perfect for a woodland garden setting. Pink, deep pink and white forms randomly planted the length of the slope transformed after the petals dropped with large, oval, orange and orangey-red hips and buttercup-yellow autumn colour. Gay would pick the hips when we were children to make rosehip syrup. Those left where enjoyed by a multitude of small birds. I replanted this hedge with Arthur in the early 1970s. In the early 1990s it was cut to ground level and all the dead wood removed. After that it was never allowed to suffer the same neglect. Petrol hedge trimmers kept it under control before the foliage broke in the spring. Rough disorderly native hedgerows grew around the north and west boundaries but these were never properly maintained. And a simple post and wire fence marked the southern edge of the plot.

The first hedge I planted in 1978, to mark out my first nursery bed by Gay's old cedar greenhouse, was of *Lonicera nitida* 'Baggesen's Gold', taking layered pieces from a huge specimen growing on the top terrace. It makes an ideal hedge especially in a sunny position where it glows bright yellow. Left as a specimen it has a loose habit of arching branches - ideal for free layers for propagation. Another line was planted the same year to hide the untidiness of Arthur's old cold frames behind his greenhouse. This was extended over the years towards the three gold conifers I planted that same year. Twelve years later this hedge would mark my newly laid out nursery on the old football pitch, where my brothers and young friends used to play. Philip removed one or two bushes later on, in order to hang a handmade gate which could be locked during garden open days.

A yew hedge was planted in front of the old swimming pool (no longer used because it leaked). A narrow sandstone wall in a state of disrepair ran along its length. The stones were removed and stacked for use elsewhere. Inexpensive paving slabs were laid against the earth; the yews planted in front. This was unsightly for a couple of years. In a narrow border running the length of the wall, Gay had grown large clumps of a glaucous-grey leaved *Echeveria* throughout the summer; these were moved back into the greenhouse before the first frosts. Yews are not slow growing if the soil is well prepared. Within a couple of seasons they concealed the slabs.

153

The deer came in one night and chewed the entire planting into interesting heights and shapes, in some places down to the main stem. I was beside myself and wished the entire herd early demise. However the yews responded well to this impromptu pruning.

Rowan (our Sussex spaniel) - young yews and paving slabs

Ten years later the hedge stood six foot high. The new growth in early spring gave a brownish tinge and when the setting sun sent its last rays across the garden the foliage would illuminate a bronze glow. This hedge provided a backdrop for a narrow curved south facing border made wider as the years progressed. As the hedge grew taller so did my confidence and my enthusiasm for herbaceous plants. The border became deeper, the grass less; the planting more prolific. The view in summer from the kitchen window was a glorious array of grasses and choice perennials. The west end planted with different shades of yellow, orange and bronze, punctuated with red and purple resembled an artist's painted canvas. A large specimen *Euphorbia nicaeensis* made a division as the planting graduated to purple, blues and reds to pink, blue and white. The Yew border was to be my one dedicated herbaceous border; although I admit I cheated just a little and added bulbs and annuals.

From the new steps on the north of the house we worked our way to the west along the top long border. This was full of grass (of the non-ornamental kind), a few perennials, a large specimen *Viburnum opulus* 'Sterile' now called *Viburnum opulus* 'Roseum' - the snowball tree. I am not sure why it was renamed 'Roseum', the balls of flowers developed from green to white until the petals fell like a snowstorm; ours had not a hint of any other colour. At the end of the border near the greenhouses a huge tank collected rainwater; this was repositioned behind the aluminium greenhouse that replaced Gay's cedar one in the late 1970s. The ancient specimen of shrubby *Lonicera syringantha* which had obscured the tank was removed and replanted on the

155

pink and white border. *L. syringantha* is a shrub with the sweetest honey fragrance in late spring and early summer. Tiny pink flowers are held in pairs from the leaf axils.

We planned a small kitchen garden near the house and greenhouses. This may have been one of the few times that we drew a plan on the back of an envelope or a scrap of paper. The remaining yew trees were planted across the end of the Yew border and beside the *Viburnum opulus*. Philip dug two tall yews from the woodland; planting them either side of the grass. My daughter Sorcha often told me that when they finally made an archway she would get married beneath it. Ten years later, with a little tying-in for encouragement, the two were joined. But by the time Sorcha was married, we were no longer living at Orchards. We took layered stems of *Lonicera nitida* 'Baggesen's Gold' from the existing hedge behind the old greenhouse to complete the outer boundaries.

Pot-bound *Hebes* grown from cuttings brought back from a trip to Wales years earlier were utilised to divide the Herb Garden from the vegetable plot. These had been destined for the bonfire. Once liberated from the confines of their pots, they grew into a wonderful

156

hedge, soft and tactile; covered in tiny white flowers in summer. Initially a wide grass path divided the two areas; however the *Hebes* grew so well that seven years later they had outgrown the space, killing the grass between. It was then that it made its way to the bonfire. The *Lonicera* hedge, planted to obscure Arthur's cold frames behind his old greenhouse and later extended, came to enclose the top nursery area and was also home for the fruit cage.

My first Herb Garden; a tiny patch, in a pocket of soil beneath the newly built sandstone wall near the kitchen door, was planted up with vibrant green curly-leaved parsley, blue-green sage, flowering chives and a froth of white-flowered thyme which trailed across the narrow ledge of moss-covered sandstone. It made a very pretty picture but was woefully inadequate for our needs. The kitchen garden took on many guises throughout our years at Orchards. When the *Hebe* hedge was removed, newly propagated boxwood was planted in its place to make a low hedge. The original design of the herb section was altered. Boxwood had been used to create compartments for growing different crops. These boxwood plants were moved to the Stump Garden.

Over the years this area was modified several times. The cedar stump; often under siege by Philip who wanted it removed against my sentimental need for it to stay; remained. We killed the grass around the stump creating a circular border, rose bay willow herb was allowed free rein - a great mistake on my part as it always succumbed to rust. Foxgloves were encouraged after I had eradicated the rose bay. I added corn marigold and ox-eye daisies; and sprinkled honesty seeds. *Hedera colchica* 'Sulphur Heart' was encouraged to scramble up and around the remains of the trunk, along with a small leaved ivy and a pale pink flowered jasmine. The grassed area - it could never truly be called a lawn - was an irregular shape and mowing was difficult where it to meet the front path. The area then evolved to become a scented garden. Three concentric circles of grass the width of the mower were retained. The rest of the turf was killed. Once dead, the soil was cultivated and mulched. Several species of *Daphne* were introduced. None thrived - there was too much shade from the surrounding ever maturing trees and shrubs. The ones that survived were moved into what later became the Pool Garden where there was more sun throughout the day and a microclimate within the confines of the yew and the copper beech hedges.

Whilst we considered how to develop this area next, I collected seed from all the different *Aquilegia* in the garden. I had been buying seed from Ray Brown - Plant World Seeds - for a few years, his additions in the 1990s were awesome; particularly the new yellow foliage introductions. The gold foliage of *Aquilegia* 'Mellow Yellow' shone in the shady borders. Another stunning *Aquilegia* 'Roman Bronze' held deep violet flowers above the yellow leaves which darkened to orange-bronze. Foliage could also be green, bluish-green, mottled green and yellow. The shapes of *Aquilegia* blooms are also varied and diverse. Long-spurred, short-spurred, spurless, clematis-flowered, doubles, pompoms. In one form or another I had a choice of them all. The seeds were mixed together and randomly scattered on the recently cleared area. The plants matured into a heart-stopping sight when flowering. Every colour and shape of blossom, every shade of foliage massed into one glorious statement. I couldn't help but smile each and every time I walked past.

However, the Stump Garden was destined to be the Herb Garden. We dug out all the mature *Aquilegia* plants, replanting them on the *Cornus kousa* border where they were never quite so happy in the poorer soil nor did they make such a statement ever again. The remaining circle of grass was removed; the soil dug and the entire area turned and cleaned of all weed and root. The irregular shape remained. Philip built a narrow concrete path along the border on the west of the house, joining both the back and front paths. The existing narrow path on the furthest side was widened where it met the front path. Philip did the same to the new path. The awkward slope of the lawn was lost behind new hardwood railway sleepers used to make a low retaining wall; leaving a narrow border which ran along the front path edge. Two shorter pieces of similar sleeper edged the newly cobbled width.

Radiating outwards from the stump, yellow paint circles were marked on the brown soil. Excitement mounted as the larger clipped boxwood - removed from the kitchen garden - were placed in a circle around the trunk, alternating between green and variegated varieties. Further circles were planted; these gradually reduced to semi-circles when the space became more limited. The two areas near the cobbled path were infilled with two mature boxwood specimens already clipped into the shape of a chicken.

The Herb Garden - the first boxwood plants in place

All of the boxwood cuttings, taken from various shrubs around the garden were inserted, as long tip cuttings with semi-hard wood around the edge of half-litre pots. I had watched this method being used at a famous boxwood nursery several years previously. Within a few weeks I had a one hundred percent take on the cuttings and was able to pot-up each individually into a one litre container.

More than three hundred and sixty little plants were set out. The stronger growing specimens interplanted with shorter ones. Small boxwood plants divided these circles and semi-circles into smaller planting areas. As these parterres grew and matured, they created a wonderfully structured feel to the area.

The Herb Garden within weeks of planting up

Copper beech was the choice to enclose the old swimming pool. A crescent was planted mirroring the shape of the newly cleared border. It was never a favourite hedge except in mid summer when the crisp brown leaves from the year before had been forced from the stems and the dark maroon foil made the perfect backdrop for the pink and white border.

162

In 1995, prior to the sale of the bungalow in which Arthur had lived for the remaining years of his life, we planted a native hedge around the boundary, finally separating it from the garden at Orchards. In many ways this hedge was the most satisfying. Composed entirely of seedlings found in abundance around the garden and in the woodland, thanks in part to the birds; a random mix of both deciduous and evergreen was planted randomly along the south and west boundaries. Even cuttings of willow pushed directly into the soil to fill the gaps took readily. Philip and I were both convinced that the increase in the number of native birds in the garden was a result of the additional hedges that we had introduced.

The Sheds

The late John Cushnie in a Sunday Telegraph piece said, *'There are lots of things a gardener needs but the two most important are patience and a shed. . .'* Arthur had both of these. A long wooden structure had been built by Arthur to house the goats during and after the war, accessed by a crude concrete path, which led from the garden gate, giving access to the farm lane on the east side of the plot, to the house, passing in front of it and on towards the sheds on the western edge. At the furthest end a lean-to protected his tools from the worst of the weather.

Spades, forks, hoes and other garden implements hung neatly from nails hammered in at different levels onto a rough plank of wood fixed to the wall. Leading off this lean-to, a small room which served as his tool shed. A handmade bench made of thick timbers, darkened with age, oil and grease, was positioned beneath the south-facing window; a vice for holding equipment in need of sharpening was fixed on one corner. Wooden shelves held small, long-necked oil cans used to get oil to the most difficult parts of all manner of machines. I remember fondly small pieces of sandpaper to clean machine plugs and oily rags tossed in untidy array in an ancient wooden tray. Old shortbread tins, golden syrup tins and tea caddies held an assortment of old bolts, screws, nuts and washers. A large wooden chest, aged with time and grease had wooden trays within, which gave a semblance of order, until they were all lifted out and the bottom revealed a jumble of ancient tools of every description.

The view down the garden was obscured by dust and cobwebs which draped from the corners of the windows. Sawdust, dirt and debris littered the windowsill. I loved the smell of this dark, dank space: of petrol cans with illfitting lids, oil spills on the concrete floor sparsely covered with sawdust. There lingered the earthy aroma of Arthur with dirty fingernails; I can still picture him giving a cursory wipe of his hands on an oily rag as Gay called him for lunch.

Along the entire length of the north wall of the sheds hung another lower roof which housed all the garden machines. The Merry Tiller cultivator which doubled up as 'the truck'; with the rotavators dissembled and a wooden trailer hitched on behind. An Allen Oxford with its scissor-like blades cut the longest grass. An assortment of other mowers; many left by different companies for Arthur's use, in the hope of a complimentary comment or article about their loan: wheelbarrows, broken trailers, oddments of wheels, rolls of netting and barbed wire, large double-handled saws hung from the rafters along with an assortment of other saws in varying sizes, and other paraphernalia of woodland gardening added to the clutter. On the eastern wall an additional low roof gave shelter to the coke for the kitchen range and logs stacked nearby for the open lounge fire.

The neighbouring sheds housed the goats in one and provided storage for the apples and pears in the other, stacked in wooden boxes; an intoxicating smell of decaying fruit mingled with the musty atmosphere. Marrows lay forgotten hardened by the frost. Large, earthy smelling hessian sacks were filled with overwintered potatoes. In the 1970s this structure was taken down and rebuilt in brick, complete with wonderful aluminium double-glazed windows; Gay's hope that they would be allowed to live in it as her arthritis worsened, was not to be. Permission was refused. In subsequent years, after us children were allocated one shed each; they became a general dumping ground. With the garden open to the public Philip refurbished Arthur's tool shed into a tea room for garden visitors.

The Caravan

What a great legacy. What a grand life this little Bluebird caravan had. I don't remember which model it was, or which year it was bought. But the one important thing about it - when it was first purchased - was that we no longer had to put up a tent in a foreign country, where the sun should be shining. But a country where it always rained; especially when we put up our grey canvas tent. They leaked if you were clumsy enough to put your head or hand on the fabric whilst the rain poured. You could then expect a steady drip until the canvas dried out. This is the caravan in which we spent many childhood holidays, travelling to Italy, France and Spain. The blue caravan was towed by a blue Bedford Dormobile which gave added sleeping - the Bluebird only slept four. I slept in the top bunk which rested precariously into two slots, making it ideal for the brother below to lift the wooden bar along the edge and tip me out.

This same caravan took Arthur and Gay around the British Isles, whilst Arthur wrote '*The Shell Guide to Gardens open to the Public*' first published in 1977. As charming and sweet as the Bluebird had been, it became redundant after Gay died. When the sheds were being rebuilt in brick; the caravan sat for a few years near the swimming pool where it was used as a changing room. From the upstairs bathroom we could see this small blue monstrosity just beyond the swimming pool. How it ever got so far from the farm lane escapes my memory, but what a dilemma. We no longer had a car with a towbar but we were determined to move it to a less conspicuous location in the garden. With a great deal of effort and a little help, Philip managed to manoeuvre it down to just below the sheds tucked away on the west boundary. It was in this position that it became a hen house. The inside was stripped out. Philip put up netting as a division, built egg boxes which could be accessed from the other side of the netting. He cut a hole in the side and built a narrow wooden 'ladder' for the hens to climb up and into the caravan. A door slotted across this hole which could be pulled up and down from the other side of the netting. A roosting pole stretched across - a pole they never used - preferring to pile one on top of the other in the egg boxes. Outside, a small area was netted and concreted in to make it fox proof. A further larger area was netted with chicken wire, for their daily scratching. A friend of ours was very disgruntled when he saw what Philip had done. He was impressed with his resourcefulness but had just seen a similar caravan sold for a lot of money as it was now considered a classic. We were pleased however to see the Bluebird's legacy live on at Orchards and to have found such an appropriate use for it in its 'retirement years'.

My Potting Shed

My potting shed was formerly the goat shed for Holly our first pygmy goat. We had selected her from a herd with the same instinct that you choose your puppy or kitten. There is generally one that appears to pick you out rather than the other way round. Holly and her herd had trotted obediently at their owners' call from the furthest edge of a ten acre field. Their colours varied from cream, black, brown and a mix of all. She had butted my hand gently and allowed me to scratch between her underdeveloped horns. She was calm when I carried her to the car and remained so, snuggled in my arms during the one hour journey back home. Arriving in darkness, we felt sad to leave her alone in her own shed, so we put her in with the hens. The following morning we took her on a collar and chain and kept her with us whilst we worked in the garden. She worked too, grazing the long neglected grass. That afternoon we introduced her to her shed - water bucket, salt lick, hay in the rack in the corner, straw on her wooden bed - which Philip had built and raised a little off the floor so she wouldn't be in a draught.

Philip had constructed this little shed on the side of the brick garage, in a type of shiplap timber with the bark retained. It blended well with the nearby woodland which became known as the Goat Wood. A netting wire fence surrounded this on three sides, with a small handmade rustic gate. Imagine our surprise when we went to put the hens away for the night, to find the little black goat back in with her newly found friends. We left her there for the time it took us to reinforce the fencing around her pen. Later we bought a second goat as a companion named Coco by Sorcha. Many people wondered why you would call a goat Coco; especially as she had named it after her favourite perfume! It was a sad day when Holly died. Coco was lonely without her company. Another little shack was built against the log shed in what now had become a major composting area. We relocated her once the shack was ready. During the day she had numerous visits from us as we barrowed garden refuse to the compost bins. Her personality improved only after Holly's death. Never very friendly and frequently a little aggressive; she mellowed once on her own; but her nuzzling was not to encourage you to scratch between her horns but as a precursor to butting you on your way out of the pen! It made composting an altogether more exhilarating experience.

And so the goats' former abode became my potting shed. Cleared out and hosed down it still seemed to have Holly's presence inside, though not her smell! Philip inserted a window - retrieved from a skip - into the original goat shed wall giving me a view down the Goat Wood. He took away the bed and built me a bench that covered nearly three sides of the building, leaving one end for the bags of compost, sand and grit to lean. There were two compost bins on these benches at right angles to each other. The one beneath the window had space nearby the door, large enough to put a small tray to take the newly potted plants. Not that it retained this use for very long as it became Saffron's favourite place to sit and gaze out of the door. Typical of a Parsons Jack Russell, Saffron was an excellent companion and kept an eye out for visitors both human and fauna. Shelves held the smaller pots and my radio. Larger pots were stacked under the benches. Philip made a latched door and hammered nails on the wall to take essential tools. I loved the earthy, dankness of this space.

My potting shed became the meeting place for family and friends. It was, especially on a rainy day, the first place they would look for me. I worked in there during the afternoon when the nursery was open. The earthen floor became solid and compacted. Philip linked in the electricity for a light and the radio but there was no space to make a cup of tea. Instead he would bring me one from the house and perch on the compost bags on his return from work and we'd chat or listen to the radio together. For the most part it was a well ordered place; given its compact size it needed to be.

One friend once watched fascinated as I prepared the 'universal' compost used for general potting. Four parts of multi-purpose compost, to one of sand and one of grit, mixed together by hand into a sandy, gritty mix. Intuitively I knew when it was correct. She asked if I made pastry with as much care. 'No', I replied 'that's chucked in the food processor and blitzed'.

A small trug which had belonged to Sorcha as a child, held the labels and pens. Another basket held the string. An old florist's vase held canes and other paraphernalia for staking. I had nails on a post to hang my coat or apron. Spent compost bags were saved for plastic rubbish or for collecting leaves for the compost bins. The potting shed became my preferred place to work; shelter from the rain; pot my plants and listen to Radio Four. The area outside was developed as the nursery sales grew. Philip constructed long benches to take the newly potted plants; to save me from bending unnecessarily. From these benches at the close of nursery business, newly potted plants would be transferred to a trailer specially adapted by Philip, to be towed by one of the tractors. From there they would be transferred to the shade and poly tunnels on the other side of the garden, to grow on until ready for sale.

The Cabin

I spent the first few years managing my nursery and serving customers, from the comfort of one of the garages that Philip had cleverly refurbished. An old office desk saved from a skip; an old kitchen chair and a shelf for the radio were the bare essentials. To these we added an old white bookcase and cupboards. A curtain which hung across the back door in Gay's kitchen at the time of her death in 1977 was used to section this area from the rear of the garage. This Sanderson fabric was an eclectic mix of late spring flowers. Bold tulips in red, yellow and mauves, weeping bluebells, curves of yellow freesia, red and mauve anemone, pheasant-eye narcissus, iris of lilac-blue and yellow trumpet daffodils. It brightened the plain walls of the garage. I could feel Gay's presence and knew that she was 'overseeing' my work. I still have an original piece of this material as a 'throw' over an antique piano stall. It has lost none of its magic. I was happy enough in this environment; except on the days when the garden was open for charity. Then the area became too small and congested.

It was obvious that we needed to expand. We searched through catalogues for a free-standing cabin. An area to the side of the selling nursery - where a decaying larch stump which had been uprooted by the 1987 hurricane was cleared and the surrounding soil levelled - made a perfect spot to place a cabin. Existing *Rhododendron ponticum* was retained and made a natural screen for the cabin from our neighbours in the bungalow. Philip had requested slight modifications to the sectional building, so that it had an overhang to the roof under which he constructed a decked area. The 'shed-type' doors were replaced with bespoke doors made by Philip. These were part wood, part glazed. The inside was lagged and boarded for extra insulation. Philip with the help of Chris Coomber, (more about him later), spent several days on its construction during the winter of 1999/2000. A beautiful curved wooden reception desk which had been stripped out during a hotel refurbishment job and skipped - then retrieved by Philip - became the new counter in my cabin. Underneath he built shelves for storage. To hide this from the public, more revamped Sanderson curtain of the same floral design was hung. Behind the counter we placed the old desk and chair and a small filing cabinet. Ever-resourceful he designed and made a display unit for my watercolour and pressed-flower cards out of more recycled wood. Arthur's writing table was set on the opposite side. A bookcase, still painted pink from my childhood bedroom, housed the necessary reference books. Underneath one of the front windows another counter was built under which was installed an old cabinet from our newly refurbished kitchen. Philip channelled electricity from the garage up to the cabin. It was now possible to make myself, visiting friends, helpers and customers a cup of tea from the luxury of my cabin. An extra touch of comfort was added - excess purple carpet tiles from an office refurbishment job carpeted the floor. On the decked veranda sat a chrome bistro table and two chairs. The cabin became my outdoor office and a fitting place to welcome visitors to the nursery and garden.

The Nursery

My wish to open a small nursery had been nurtured and nourished for years. Long before I did so I had propagated for friends and family, sold plants at school fetes and at a local farm shop. By the middle of 1992, I had propagated sufficient stock to start my business. My initial inclination, given the name of Arthur's legacy, was to name it Orchards Nursery. However when my first wholesale consignment of flowerpots was delivered to another similar sounding nursery in the same area I realised that I had no choice but to reconsider my options. Hellyer's Garden Plants was the title I opted for. I had already stopped working full time to help care for Arthur and to undertake the garden work that he was no longer able to do. The nursery had only opened for a couple of weekends before Arthur's health problems took a more serious turn. I chose to focus my energies on his care and making him comfortable, so I closed up and I did not reopen until the following March - several weeks after his passing.

From humble beginnings the nursery evolved. Nearby the garden gate Philip had built a series of compartments using old railway sleepers. This was an excellent, if rustic place to set plants for sale. Ground

176

cover was laid to stop the weeds and grass growing. Wood chippings were used to create wide pathways between each. A long shaded area, netted across the top of one long compartment, ran parallel to the driveway. The recycled sleepers quickly proved unsuitable as they leeched an oily substance. Concerned they would stain a customer's clothing or shoes; they were removed and reused elsewhere in the garden. Philip then laid out standing areas covered with pea shingle, divided by green netting to give some degree of shade. In later years long benches replaced these; over which struts were built to take shading if necessary during the summer months. This was mainly for my benefit. My health was deteriorating and bending and kneeling was becoming more difficult.

The nursery was my joy. It was an ambition fulfilled. None of it would have been possible without the support of Philip. The long hours and hard work were a pleasure - at least for me. It kept me within the place I most loved; with an ever increasing number of herbaceous plants for which I had a passion.

Hardy *Geraniums* became a speciality for the nursery, at one time selling more than one hundred different varieties; so many of the species being the perfect plant for a woodland setting. They were increasing in popularity during the 1990s and in early 2000s. I bought most of my stock plants from one of the leading authorities of the time David Hibberd, who wrote a RHS Wisley Handbook on the subject. Inscribed in my copy is *'To Penny, Many thanks for your help, Love David'*. This informative book is still a firm favourite.

The nursery layout in 2004

I introduced several cultivars of my own. *Geranium* x *oxonianum* 'Rosemary Verey', a striking plant with large, well marked pink flowers and blue-green foliage. *Geranium nodosum* 'Saucy Charlie' after my daughter Sorcha, whose second name is Charlotte. Saucy Charlie was the name that Gay gave her as a small child.   And a *Geranium pratense* seedling by default. At a local flower show I sold two *Geranium pratense* seedlings to Graham Spencer of Croftway Nursery who also specialised in hardy *Geranium*.   He was so enamoured with them both that he asked if he could name them and if so what would I like them to be called.   One had lilac buds which opened palest lilac with dark stamens this would be Arthur Hellyer; the other with pink buds that opened to palest pink would be Gay Hellyer.   This was the one that Graham introduced.   It is still for sale today.   My love for hardy *Geraniums* also led me to be, if only briefly, the Hardy Geranium Society Newsletter editor - a job I loved.

As the nursery flourished, Philip made delightful wooden 'trugs' from left-over timber.   These were to carry selected purchases in.   He also constructed another long bench outside the nursery for customers to assemble their chosen treasures.   Although it was a small nursery, many customers said that selecting from my choice specimens was a dilemma.   Certainly seeing plants in situ at Orchards was inspiring for many visitors and I was always happy to give advice when asked.

Rosemary Verey had sent me a list of 'must have' plants to grow for the nursery. Hardy *Geranium, Penstemon* and *Salvia* were high on the list. A number of *Salvias* were purchased from Elizabeth Strangman's excellent nursery at Hawkhurst, in Kent - now sadly closed. Several other genera of plants became important to the nursery. *Campanula* is such a diverse family, with plant species that cover a range of planting situations. *Aster* was another that gave good autumn colour to the garden. *Anthemis, Achillea, Coreopsis,* or indeed any of the many species within the daisy family became firm favourites. When ornamental grasses became popular, my collection of them in the garden and then on the nursery benches grew in number annually. I made several special borders for them; as well as using them within mixed plantings - allowing visitors to see the different ways in which they could be used, this in turn lead to greater sales. I propagated ninety-nine percent of the sale material myself, taking cuttings, making divisions or growing from seed throughout the year. If the weather was particularly cold or inclement for gardening or propagating, then I would work in the cabin, either making pressed flower cards, painting cards for sale, catching up on indexing or adding to my list of 'must have' plants.

I loved those eleven years; in many ways the most rewarding of my life. I especially enjoyed the small garden groups who would come, sometimes with a picnic, and spend time within the garden. Many very overwhelmed that they were in the garden of the late Arthur Hellyer. Several customers gifted copies of Arthur's books to me. Whilst others asked me to sign the inside cover for them. One guy - an actor whose name I have forgotten - called one day when the nursery was first opened and asked if he could purchase a log from an apple tree laying in the orchard that Philip had recently thinned. He wanted it for his patio in his London garden. He returned on the first day we opened for the National Gardens Scheme - earlier than the official opening time, walked round the garden with a friend and left a more than generous donation for the charity.

For the last few years of the nursery opening we did a mail order service too; which proved very successful. For the most part I met some very nice people through the garden openings and nursery. Quite a number regularly came back year after year to see the garden's evolution or to stock up on yet more treasures for their own gardens.

Greenhouses and Tunnels

My adult gardening life began with one greenhouse; a twenty-fourth birthday present from Arthur and Gay. By the age of forty-one I was surrounded by greenhouses and tunnels and I had managed to fill them all in one way or another; as well as the cold frames that Philip had rebuilt for me on the side of Arthur's former greenhouse. The oldest cold frames behind had remained more or less intact. Sadly Gay's cedar greenhouse had rotted over time and had been replaced with an aluminium one in the late 1970s. Philip's occupation as a carpenter, often working for companies who wanted their offices stripped out and refitted, gave us a constant supply of useful material to be used at Orchards, - which would otherwise have been skipped. So the greenhouse he built for me was extra special and quite unique, recycling bits and pieces discarded by others. This new greenhouse was built adjacent to the aluminium one. The site for this was further down the slope. Instead of levelling the area he built a brick plinth from reject West Hoathly brick higher on the slope side. This made a level base for the aluminium and dark tinted glass from an office refurbishment job. It was a variation on an old theme and fitted in well at Orchards. A central path was dug and concreted just as in Arthur's old greenhouse, with two concrete walls to hold the soil. These walls were made a little wider, so, if necessary the tractor could be driven onto them for maintenance work to be done with access from underneath.

Along one side ran a wood-framed polythene propagation unit, divided in the middle with a piece of wood; one half of which was heated by cable under the sand. On the opposite side an area for pots to stand; above which a metal pole with hooks took hanging baskets. At the top of this central path two areas were concreted. On one side were stacked bags of compost and grit, on the other a space to mix compost. The double patio-type doors were also saved from a skip.

Large hoops - extracted by us from under years of bramble growth - had been bought from a local farmer for a few pounds and reinstated on the old football pitch. The entire area was laid with black membrane to suppress the grass and the weeds. Two poly tunnels stood side by side, one longer than the other. The longest was later covered with shading. There was space for pots in between. Philip made the doors for both. This was now the top nursery; used for propagation and the growing on of stock, as opposed to the selling nursery. Eventually the entire area had to be fenced to keep out curious garden visitors and the ever persistent rabbits and deer.

Cedar Veranda

I have old black and white photos which show no veranda when the house was first built in the 1930s. As a child I remember a Crittall sunroom, glazed on three sides set against the wooden wall of the house. Lidded benches ran under the front windows, in which were kept the Wellington boots and garden shoes. I hated this area; as I was very squeamish about spiders and insects that moved rapidly. In the late 1960s Gay and Arthur replaced these with benches that would hold Gay's collection of bulbs and indoor plants. Her old oak table was placed in here, where on inclement days she would prepare vegetables or sit and work for Arthur. By the early 1990s the structure was rusted through and in a state of collapse. The glass door had to be kicked open and kicked from the other side to close.

With the garden open to the public it had become an unacceptable eyesore. We resolved to remove it completely and build a new cedar veranda in keeping with the house. With care Philip cut the metal framed sections up into smaller pieces and skipped them. The wired glass roof panels were retained and reduced in size; cutting away the cracks. The depth of the new veranda was determined by the length he could make these good. In just a few weeks the structure was complete. New cedar posts supported the wired glass roof and the additional floor space that had not been utilised was filled with soil and used as an external raised border in front of the veranda. Originally we had it in mind to glaze in between the posts but decided against it. The cedar soon mellowed to blend perfectly with the house.

Sandstone Walls

The first project Philip undertook after we met in 1989 was the rebuilding of the sandstone wall on the north side of the house. This area was altered quite drastically before the wall was rebuilt. A large patio was dug out and paved; old narrow sandstone steps removed and new wider curved steps built with sandstone pavers, which lead towards the top garden.

In late 1993, with the first opening of the garden planned for May the following year, we set to. The front of the house was a disgrace. A square patio had been laid on the old heather garden in the late 1970s, with an ugly retaining wall built with inferior red brick which was out of place - an awkward square jutting out into the grass. The brickwork was in a state of decay. Some of it was falling down, but the rest proved too difficult to remove. Ever resourceful we decided to reface the wall - taking sandstone from the swimming pool border, the wall on the northwest side of the house - which was replaced with chestnut stakes wired together to bolster and strengthen it. This border, divided into two levels became known as the Chestnut Terrace - and other sandstone which had been set aside.

We agreed that the squareness should be lost; curves were created on either side. To the west, the wall was taken further out and then rounded to meet the existing border. This area was filled in with the soil that we had retained when the back patio had been dug out. On the east side a curved planting area linked back in with the existing long border. On the west side two steps took you down to a lower terrace. Having crossed the terrace, one further step took you back up along a short newly created path to the concrete pathway in front of the Stump Garden. Both of these terraced areas were covered with membrane over which we raked tons of pea shingle.

The border on the east was edged with smaller pieces of sandstone. This border was originally a 'grey garden'. One of the few grasses in the garden from when I was a child, *Helictotrichon sempervirens* the Blue Oat grass, was planted prominently in the centre. Around it were planted an eclectic mix of grey leaved plants - *Anaphalis triplinervis, Artemisia absinthium, A. ludoviciana* 'Silver Queen', *Lychnis coronaria seedlings* with varying shades of magenta flowers, *Nepeta* 'Six Hills Giant', *Amsonia orientalis* with its starry blue flowers and other sun loving gems.

It was the Blue Oat grass with its long flower stems arching from low blue-grey foliage which gave us the idea of making a grass garden on this border. On one of those rare days when we found time to sit out on the veranda, the flower stems looked so graceful, waving in the slight breeze. My most favourite plant in this border was a low growing thyme which Rosemary Verey had given me labelled 'thyme from Scotland'. This delightful prostrate plant scrambled over the little wall, across the edge of the border and crept stealthily onto the pea shingle. Its tiny bluish-grey leaves were awash with bluish-pink flowers every summer, smothered with visiting bees. We left it to meander.

In its second life the 'grey garden' became one of the grass gardens. Any misgiving that I may have had about its placement completely disappeared one dull Christmas Day morning. Catching a glimpse out of the stair window at the buff beauties still glowing against the greyness, was enough to make me reflect on just how much pleasure this garden had given me throughout the year. The curved border edged with sandstone was approximately eleven feet at the widest point, two feet at one end and five at the other. Planted with different species of *Stipa*, *Luzula*, *Pennisetum*, *Panicum*, *Uncinia*, *Festuca* and *Carex* to name but a few - the grasses melded and grew well but by the end of the first year we had to reassess the planting. We set an ultimate height of four foot - gleaned from the descriptions taken from a couple of grass catalogues and one excellent grass book '*The Plantfinder's Guide to Ornamental Grasses*' written by Roger Grounds. Some of the grasses had grown to more than four feet in height and were too dense in their habit, blocking the spectacular view down the southern vista.

Initially we moved *Miscanthus sinensis* 'Undine' - probably my favourite *Miscanthus* with greenish leaves and a central white rib, yellowing with age - and *Eragrostis curvula,* into different positions within the garden. The following season others were moved to the two new grass borders we had made in the top arboretum; whilst the low growing grasses were reorganised to give a more pleasing colour association.

The front of the house in 2003

Despite the fact that *Miscanthus* take a long time to raise their beautiful plumes and that some of the grasses are deciduous, the effect seen on Christmas morning

189

was breathtaking So many shades of beige, the flowers, some bold and solid, some open and airy.

Seedlings of *Lavandula angustifolia* 'Hidcote' were planted in front of the undulating sandstone wall. Tones of deep purple and paler lilac lit the area. The curved border to the west was planted with hardy *Geraniums* which preferred part shade and appropriate shrubs and shade loving plants.

Paths, Steps and Bridges

Where should a path go? Anywhere that your feet take you, we decided. Philip had watched me nip across two particular borders; one giving me a shortcut to the greenhouses, the other from the long front border to the kitchen path. He dug both out for me. The greenhouse path was concreted and the levels of soil held back with narrow logs wired together to strengthen. The other was laid with reclaimed pavers infilled with sand and cement with two railway sleeper steps down. Woodland paths were cut closely with a narrow gauge mower, meandering between the raised roots of the trees and bushes, covered with wood chippings when available. After a couple of years when the chippings had composted down, they were removed and used as mulch and fresh chippings were laid.

New and old railway sleepers were used for all manner of construction. They were an inexpensive and more subtle option for a woodland garden. Several were bolted together to make retaining walls to hold back the excess soil of the little borders in front of the cabin; which contained part of my hardy *Geranium* collection. More were utilised to retain the soil for the new *Iris* beds around the recently filled in swimming pool; and for the steps. Out of necessity a ditch was dug (more about this later) two thirds of the way down the front vista; across this Philip made a bridge from three new sleepers. He also constructed a bridge across the pond from two old telegraph poles left lying in the garden. His resourcefulness knew no bounds.

The Cartwheel Bench

Impulsiveness is not a quality I would attribute to my husband, but on returning one Saturday morning from an agricultural retailer with a tractor part we needed, he discussed the seat he had seen in the shop and wondered if I thought we should buy it. From his description it sounded interesting and unusual, but expensive. The back of the bench was constructed from one cartwheel; the curved arms and other supports from parts of an old hay cart.

191

'It's up to you,' I said - which he knew I would.

'Good,' he replied, 'Because I bought it. It's for the decking outside your cabin.'

The seat didn't make it to the decking. Instead, we decided to put it up out of the sight of the farm lane until we could work out some way to secure it to the decking. It must be said that it was so heavy; I doubt anyone would have been able to move it easily but there it stayed for several years tucked nicely into a bank of *Rhododendron ponticum*. We would sit with a cup of tea, basking in the evening sun and enjoy the view along the back long border. I was pleased to see a similar bench at Chelsea Flower Show a couple of years later costing much more money that Philip had parted with.

Its final placement at Orchards was in the Pool Garden - here you could enjoy the setting sun - whilst watching gold finches and tits weave in and out of the white, pink and red cosmos; which had grown so tall that they could also be viewed from the bathroom window waving above the yew hedge.

A couple of teak garden benches bought second-hand replaced white plastic ones donated by a friend. Solid, well built and aged to a warm grey hue; one was placed on the lower terrace to view the front vista, the other outside the outbuildings, where tea and cake would be served to garden visitors.

The Cartwheel Bench in the Pool Garden

In the wooded area below the *Catalpa*, Philip constructed one wooden bench from two sturdy logs with the seat made from a plank of a felled trunk. This was placed in the shelter of some conifers with a close view of the corky trunk of *Sequoiadendron giganteum* and with the heady scent of *Azalea mollis* in spring and bluebells in May.

A grey concrete seat placed on two concrete squirrels was like a horror story to me. I hated it with a vengeance; but what could you do? It was a fiftieth birthday present from one of our girls. The greyness was transformed with the leftovers of a can of National

Trust Green; which in time developed spider-vein cracks giving a crackle glazed effect. Only then did the seat blend nicely with the sandstone walls of the back patio.

Statues

I had bought a concrete statue of a Grecian lady one day in the early 1970s. She stood naked, coyly covering her right breast with a drape of fabric. Her head slightly bowed towards her left shoulder. Long hair coiled and curled into an elegant style. It was her grace that made me fall in love with her. I loved her even more when she faded, blotched in lighter and darker patches of grey, a shadow of ochre lichen aged her forehead and face. She blended so much better with the surrounding plants.

We added a few more concrete statues to the garden over the years. I bought a cherub birdbath, the bowl of which was broken some years later. A brass sundial was purchased for him to hold instead. Philip bought me a pair of concrete Wellington boots and, with the help of a pot of live yogurt it didn't take long for moss and lichen to age them. I filled the boots with gravel mixed with a scant amount of soil into which I planted the common houseleek *Sempervivum tectorum* in either one, the blue-green leaves often turning red-purple when under stress.

An owl, wings outstretched, moulded in a sandy-coloured concrete made a statement within an ancient *Cotoneaster* which Philip had trimmed closely into a rounded shape. The neglected growth in the front of this shrub was cut away to reveal a filigree network of branches. The owl sat on a rectangle of sandstone as if about to take flight.

The owl waiting to fly

For Christmas one year I purchased a large statue of an Easter Island man which Philip had admired in the local garden centre. A guy at the centre helped me manhandle it onto a trolley - it lay prostrate, its stern gaze upward facing whilst I waited in line at the cash desk. 'Oh look mummy,' a little voice cried, 'that looks just like daddy's face!' Philip's face was one of joy when he pulled off the cardboard box under which I had hidden it.

When Philip had finished my two new scree beds, set on either side of the steps to the east lawn; I introduced 'marbled cobbles'. These large rounded cobbles were pattered terracotta and sandy-yellow. They looked wonderful with the racemes of azure blue flowers of *Veronica austriaca* 'Ionian Skies'; its dark green ferny foliage lax in habit. The bluish-green basal leaves of *Alchemilla erythropoda* contrasted sharply with lime green cymes. There grew an eclectic mix of different alpine plants. *Alchemilla alpina*; its pretty, tactile, deep green leaves backed with velvety silver hairs. Numerous low-growing hardy *Geraniums* with varied coloured foliage were added. Several cultivars of *G. renardii* could be viewed easily on the raised scree. All had sage green rounded, divided, wrinkled leaves with a soft texture. *G. r.* 'Tcschelda' with its upward facing lilac-blue flowers veined purple was looser in habit. *G* 'Bertie Crûg' gave a strong contrast. From mounds of bronze foliage crept stems with small deep pink flowers over a long period. *G* 'Black Ice' made another dark bronzed statement, with small white flowers. The ash-grey foliage of *G. cinereum* and its cultivars provided a different tone; the flower colours in hues of purplish-pink, dark-veined with dark central zones. The foliage of *G. orientalitibeticum* was strongly marbled green-yellow with purplish-pink flowers and a white centre. It wandered around producing chains of small tubers and could be invasive but was easily propagated.

The numerous star-shaped, pale pink flowers marked with purple midribs of *Allium karataviense* hung in umbels over a long layered splinter of slate picked up from the roadside in Andorra. The deep grey stone changed to charcoal grey after rain. A chunk of white quartz, taken from a Welsh mountainside during my travels with Arthur after Gay's death, glittered in the sunlight.

When driftwood became fashionable in the 1990s, I carried one piece back from Hampton Court Flower Show as a present for Philip. 'It looks like a canine tooth,' a colleague remarked. I was never quite as fond of it after that. But I did like the texture of the wood and the changes in colour when wet or dry.

Chapter Six

Foes of the Garden

Foes fell into three categories. The first, small, slimy and devious; this category included wireworms, leatherjackets, cockchafer grubs, vine weevil and their larvae, slugs and snails, lily beetles, horseflies, midges, leafhoppers, hornets and wasps. The second were furry and feathery; in this category: fox, rabbit, deer, squirrels, moles, voles, mice, magpies and pheasants. The third was vegetative; and included honey fungus and pernicious weeds.

Moss should have been counted as a foe too, had I been a better gardener. We had lots of sphagnum moss in the grass; especially in the top arboretum where the soil was damper. But we loved to see the birds stripping it from the grass for use in their nests. I used it for lining the hanging baskets which I made up every year for customers and myself. Once, after criticism from a garden visitor, I raked the east lawn to try to eradicate the moss. It was the most disheartening job I had ever undertaken. I also tried a chemical option which relied on rain within a specified time; or you had to hose the lawn. The rain didn't come and the hose didn't quite stretch far enough. We were left with a very ugly blackened lawn for quite some time. We resigned ourselves to accepting this 'invasion', appreciating is spongy, springy presence.

In Arthur's day, leatherjackets and wireworms were the soil pests he would most likely find in the garden. He taught me to chop leatherjackets cleanly and quickly with secateurs and to snap wireworms by holding them between your index finger and thumb on both hands and giving a quick twist. Leatherjackets, the larvae of the crane fly are typically seen in early autumn. Mating and egg laying occurs within twenty-four hours of the emergence of the crane fly. The females drop to the ground and insert one egg at a time into the soil. The eggs hatch within a few weeks and the larvae remain under the soil for a year, feeding on the roots of plants and burying into various tubers. On wet nights they sometimes emerge and eat the stems as well. Their dark grey colour is a good camouflage for them in the borders. They are like a legless caterpillar, wriggling from side to side to bury themselves once exposed. It probably explained the presence of the numerous different bird species which pecked away on the grass throughout the garden. Other predators included foxes

199

and badgers would dig for the grubs. Around the garden, divots were removed by either badgers or foxes. We never actually saw a badger in the garden but we did find a badger latrine in the top woodland.

The stiff-bodied, orangey-yellow wireworm moves very slowly if unearthed. It can spend as long as four years underground, tunnelling into potato, carrot and other root crops; feeding on plant roots and the bases of soft stems. After pupating for three weeks, they emerge as adult click beetles in the summer. This beetle has a brown elongated body and feeds on plant tissue, pollen and nectar. In May and June, the female lays eggs in weedy ground, although we often found them in well cultivated soil. Most of my gardening days were spent in the company of a robin or our little bantam hens, who saved me the trouble of snapping the wireworms in half. Once unearthed the robin would dive in and out for a quick feast. In Arthur's book *'Garden Pest Control'* his organic recommendation was to slice carrot or potato, fix it to wooden skewers and bury them just beneath the surface; examine daily and destroy any wireworms found.

Chafer grubs are the larvae of the chafer beetle. The large beetles fly in a cumbersome laboured way in May at dusk, often bumping into things or people as they go. Gay fell from her bicycle one evening, when a beetle smacked into her forehead as she cycled along the farm lane. The grubs develop from the eggs which are laid deep in the earth in April and May; once pupated they lay beneath the soil for three years or more, eating plant roots including potato; causing damage to a diverse range of plants before emerging as adults. The adults chomp on the leaves of deciduous trees - oak is a favourite. Although they are harmless to humans; they neither sting nor bite, though their awkward flight can be a little unnerving. If unearthed the large creamy-white grubs; with brownish-orange heads and a darker hue around their swollen abdomens lay in a 'c' shape rarely moving. In colder areas they may be in the soil for a longer period, burying even deeper below the surface. The adults overwinter beneath ground too, at up to a depth of one metre.

Very few vine weevil larvae were found in the soil in the 1970s. By the end of the 1980s they were the most common pest, followed by leatherjackets then wireworms. The vine weevil larvae were loved by the robins, our chickens and our dog Saffron (not necessarily a good idea as she could sniff them out and start digging if you were not observant at all times). Pheasants can detect them as well. In autumn, the female pheasants sheltering in our garden from the gamekeeper, who had bred them for the shoot in neighbouring woodland, would cause chaos in the top nursery area, pecking and digging in both the ground and in the pots, toppling them in their search for the larvae. A positive attitude was adopted.

One adult vine weevil beetle - they are all female - can lay between five and sixteen hundred small, pearl-like eggs either on the host plant or on the surface of the soil, over a two month period. I never found them at this stage; the eggs darken with age to brown and then into small creamy-white grubs with an orangey-brown head. They too nestle in a 'c' shape like the chafer grub, buried in the soil chewing on the roots or burrowing into the rootstock or tuber. Sometimes they overwinter in a pre-pupating stage. They look very alien at this phase as they fatten out losing their grub like appearance; with close inspection tiny black 'pinheads' can be seen which denotes the forming of their eyes.

Great satisfaction was gained by destroying the grey adults. The beetle may, by nature, be nocturnal but I had worked far too hard through the day to want to go out at night and wait for them. The observant gardener once familiar with their appearance can detect them with ease. Sometimes they would be found at the bottom of a plant pot as you lifted it. Often they were just underneath the rim of the pot, tucked down nice and snugly into the surface soil near the top. I used to put the pot down and wait. Once still, they would move off slowly to another hiding place! My patience would invariably pay off. Occasionally they even had the temerity to come indoors - climbing up the ivy and through the bathroom window.

In the nursery I did try a chemical control for a few seasons which was very expensive and seemed to be of little use. Diligence was the only answer - the pots were inspected frequently - any grubs removed and fed to the robins; the roots washed with a much diluted mix of Jeyes fluid and water, then repotted. Someone once told me that good beetles and insects run away when disturbed, those up to no good, play dead in the hope that you will go away. Though I didn't like killing any living creature, practicality took over. I did have a problem crushing snails and was squeamish enough not to slice large slugs in two with a pair of secateurs. A bucket of saline water was the answer. Once I collected a bucketful of snails without saline water, thinking they would make a nice treat for the hens. I returned with a barrow load of weeds for the hens some minutes later to find an escargatoire of snails on their way back through the netting. Slugs did, I think, do less harm than snails, the slugs concentrating more on the dead, decaying matter, although I once found one large orange slug devouring the new growth of a *Campanula,* 'jaws' opened like a vice. I would find lots of snails hiding beneath the leaves of *Hemerocallis* in particular, where they could easily be picked off by hand.

After a brief flip through Arthur's book *'Garden Pests and Diseases'*, I decided only to use it as a reference book. Experience taught me that whatever plant you introduced into your garden, the relevant pest and disease may well follow. No lily beetle had been noted on the oldest lilies planted by Gay in the 1960s. It was twenty years later when I purchased new lily bulbs that these little red devils came to my notice. Then it was a non-gardening friend who drew my attention to them; she having the time to read the garden magazines.

Lily bulbs in pots had been placed in glorious array on the back steps for my admiration from the kitchen window. My daughter Sorcha drew my attention to the brown blobs on the leaves of the lilies - she was supposed to be studying in the sunshine but the heady fragrance from the lilies had momentarily distracted her. I informed her with great assurance that these were droppings. As a young child I had shown her caterpillar droppings left on the leaves of cabbages. She accepted this statement and chose to ignore my request to remove the leaves if they caused her offence. 'Did you know they move?' she called a few minutes later. This made me refer to Arthur's book and to my horror I discovered that the eggs laid on the reverse of the foliage, develop into pupae, which then live within their own excreta, safe in the knowledge that they would be left alone. Not on my patio! I would prefer a naked stem to any more lily beetles. From that moment, I was diligent in my observations for and removal of, the clusters of red eggs, the larvae and the adults (which by some stroke of luck I often found them in twos). Don't be fooled by them playing dead. Place one hand under the leaf on which these crafty beetles stand; the slightest shadow makes them drop, always on their backs. They are brilliant scarlet above, with black head and legs, and jet black beneath. Within seconds they turn turtle - squash firmly between the thumbnail and your forefinger. If they fall to the ground, move a little but stay transfixed, you are left with a second chance. Feel no remorse.

It is interesting that there is no mention of the lily beetle in either the 1944 copy of Arthur's *'Garden Pest Control'* or in the 1966 edition of Arthur's *'Garden Pests and Diseases'*. Early January and February is a good time to look for foes. When dividing *Leucantheum* in early January, I discovered several lily beetles basking in the early sunlight amongst the low basal growth. With milder winters, greenfly and whitefly could also be detected.

I would notice wasps from early spring feeding from *Aubrieta* and other spring flowering plants. I understand that many would consider them friends not foes because they are important pollinators and useful predators. But I hated wasps. I had many childhood memories of them becoming entangled in my long hair; and occasionally Arthur would be seen running across the lawn trying to simultaneously take off his trousers after he'd disturbed a wasp nest whilst gardening.

Every year, without fail, they would make numerous nests under the eaves of the house and or in the attic at the furthest corner, in the area that wasn't boarded. They could be seen stripping pieces from the cedar shingle roof and cladding or from the hardwood garden seats. It may not have mattered so much if the house hadn't been dressed with so many climbers but by August any pruning became a real hazard.

One year when Sorcha was very small we returned from our summer holiday to find her bedroom covered in dead or dying wasps. They littered her bed, the carpet, the chest of drawers, the windowsill and a few were weakly trying to exit through the closed windows. The nest under the apex of the north extension had gone unnoticed. They had increased the size of their nest by chewing into and through the soft boarding of the ceiling. Having come in they couldn't find their way out. I can still recall the putrid odour of decaying dead wasps. The material bag of the vacuum cleaner smelt fetid for months after they had been hoovered up.

Wasps would become most problematic in the late summer and early autumn, when they became lethargic and aggressive as they sought out sweet things to eat. In the orchards they ate into the good apples still on the trees and on the ground where the rotting flesh of the windfalls made them tipsy with fermenting juice. In the summer of 2004 several nests were found in the garden underground - a sign of a hot summer I was had been told. More than once I pushed the little mower over a wasp nest made in an old rabbit hole in the woodland. This would send me sprinting across the grass, with goosebumps the size of boils on my arms; the mower abandoned, the engine left idling; where it remained until it had run out of fuel.

In 2004, hornets were becoming increasingly troublesome. Many large nests hung from the *Camellia* bushes in the top woodland, making grass cutting very hazardous. We had these removed by a professional but the largest one was found in the attic. Philip cut it from the roof joist with a knife and slid it into a large black rubbish sack; with just enough room left over to tie the top!

Grubbing in the earth or at least at ground level is a very good form of pest control. Even the trained eye misses some devils from above, but down there with them, the light falls differently. Aphids collecting on stems of *Lupinus arboreus* were a bluish-green. They were enormous. From above they appeared so still, down in their world their movements were constant as they steadily sucked the sap from the stems. I still use Gay's method of control - a solution of washing-up liquid diluted with water and a little vinegar, sprayed at dusk, or on a cloudy day.

In the 1990s I gardened accompanied by two partridge-coloured Dutch bantam hens and their cockerel - in my opinion the only acceptably sized cockerel to keep. They were free-range in the truest sense of the word. He was a very handsome little bird, gaily coloured black, green and orange, with a curved tail and scarlet comb. He took very good care of his ladies. They followed me along the borders pecking in the newly trowelled soil - he was closest to me. When he found something worth eating he would cluck to his ladies and stamp his little feet; allowing them first pickings. He regularly brought his 'girls' into the kitchen to inspect where we lived.

I couldn't abide gardening whilst being bitten by midges or attacked by horseflies. I had lived at Orchards for more than forty-five years before I learnt the hard way that there was more than one type of biting fly. Plagued as a child by a greyish, flat-bodied horsefly who buzzed with extreme friendliness around my head - it was one action that could set me running frantically around the garden; or if dressed accordingly a huge leap into the swimming pool would keep them at bay. Gay pointed out that this was the male and that he meant no harm. It is the female who bites, with jaws developed to penetrate the coat of a horse or cattle; therefore on more delicate human skin there is no resistance. They are light-footed, often settling out of reach to draw blood. Once bitten, an angry hard swelling would develop. Cleansing the area quickly was important as the horsefly could carry bacteria from other animals. Keeping the area cool, if redness developed, and applying an antihistamine cream, frequently helped. If one settled when I was in company I would invite my companion to slap me. A deceased horsefly is better than one which can sneak behind you and bite on another occasion. Poor Philip was never so lucky. Most of his bites occurred while he was on the tractor cutting the grass. They would find the exposed, often slightly fattier parts of the body; within minutes an angry redness surrounded the raised lump. It was Philip who 'introduced' me to the other kind of biting fly. Dive bombed by an aerodynamic fly with emerald eyes; (which I now know to be *Chrysops relictus* - the deer fly), we watched fascinated as it landed on his arm - until it bit him. He was left with a small but very solid lump beneath the skin, the puncture mark visible to the naked eye.

Midges were just a nuisance; a hat would keep most from the head area but they would find another succulent place to nip. Tee-tree oil wiped around the neck and on the backs of the hands deterred them to an extent. Leafhoppers were rife; particularly on *Rhododendron ponticum*; although chemical treatment was available we didn't use any in the garden unless it was absolutely essential. Chemicals are not selective; we would have solved the leafhopper issue but in doing so we could also have killed many of their predators. Instead we grew plants that encouraged predatory flies; *Coreopsis,* dill, fennel and *Salvia* as well as other nectar rich plants.

It is a common myth that foxes kill just for fun. It isn't so. With cubs to feed and a surplus of easy food to be found in your chicken run it made perfect sense for the fox to slaughter all and come back over a period of time to cache their prey. For us the loss of our 'girls' and 'boys' was very personal and, despite our best endeavours, all too frequent. The fox is a determined, agile, intelligent animal. The wire netting area attached to the hen house was dug in and cemented on three sides; with a narrow wire netting gate. Over the top of this area further plastic netting was draped and tied at intervals to make it secure. On this occasion fox had climbed the side netting and pushed its way under the top netting, jumping down and into the hen house on one of those rarest of summer days when we hadn't dropped the little door down. At 5am the next day - on one of our NGS open days - I had started to clean and tidy at the tea room, opposite the hen house. It took me a few moments to realise that I couldn't hear the gentle thump to the ground as they piled out of their egg boxes, squawking in their impatience to be let out. Their normal cluck-cluck greeting was absent. I opened the caravan door. There was no sign of a hen. Looking through the netting door of the small run I was almost sick with the sight of the carnage before me. Nearly every hen was dead. One or two were very badly damaged around the neck. Only one Welsummer hen remained intact and in shock. She was still installed in one of the egg boxes. Two were missing. It took a while to find the hole through which the fox had exited, the wire had been bitten and pushed through with signs of Speckledy hen feathers hooked on the netting. We had lost hens to the fox before but never on such a scale. Philip had to deal with the maimed hens when he joined me in the garden. We left the remaining Welsummer locked in the henhouse for the rest of the day. The slaughter of the morning was hidden from the view of the garden visitors. We couldn't eat chicken for months; the sight of their creamy-white flesh fresh in our minds. We took the loss badly but it didn't deter us from buying more hens. Unfortunately the fox nearly always managed to take our hens no matter how secure we made them. They were an easy target. Many times after I had shut the 'girls' away in the evening I would look across the garden to see the fox sitting at the bottom of the slope; head tilted upwards smelling me.

When one of our bantam hens became broody, a farmer friend Peter gave us a motley clutch of eggs - a random selection from the different breeds that he sold - for her to hatch. The colours of the emerging chicks were as diverse as the collected eggs; black, brown, white and yellow. One of these became a firm favourite - a pure white Silkie, with fluffy silky feathers, blue earlobes, and five instead of the normal four toes per foot. She had a comical look; from her tufty head to her feathery feet. When they were still chicks, Rowan, our Sussex spaniel, once waddled down to where we were gardening - her slobbery mouth drooping open. We could hear chirrups; we looked around but we could see nothing. Rowan sat nearby her head hanging down; a mournful expression in her eyes. We could still hear chirping. She let her mouth fall open. Inside were two of the chicks, held softly inside her cheeks. She dropped them on command and we scooped them up and ran to the coop. One small part of the netting had been chewed through. Maybe the fox had been interrupted in its task. With all the chicks safely back inside, we left the coop inside the shed and rushed to the farmer to buy narrower dimensioned netting which we swiftly used to replace the old. Sadly it wasn't their only encounter with danger and the next time they weren't so lucky. The chicks once grown and gardening with me were slaughtered by a fox in the five minutes it took me to make a cup of tea. The only remains found were a trail of white Silkie feathers up through the woodland.

My delightful Dutch bantams were taken one night from the triangle coop that Philip had made them. They lived within the fenced off top nursery. The coop was small enough for them to sleep in, with a modest amount of netting run for them peck in if they were not out in the garden with me. Most days we were gardening together, like new puppies they were never far from my side. The door of the coop was secured with swivel catches and a large piece of concrete leant against it. The door to the run was also weighted down with a large stone tied to a piece of rope. To lift it you pulled the stone up, to secure you allowed it to drop. Incredibly this fox not only pulled on the rope to lift up the stone, it dug frantically around the coop to excavate underneath then nosed or pushed the concrete out of the way. Deeply gouged scratch marks on the outside of the door showed its frenzied attempt to get in - which it did - a true feat of determination. All three were gone with barely a feather to show for any fight they may have put up.

Of course Mr Fox could have eaten the plentiful rabbits in the garden instead of my hens but I guess their zigzag run across the garden made them a more difficult meal to secure. Saffron caught baby rabbits quite often, though I suspect for a Parsons Jack Russell, it was more the thrill of the chase than the 'meal' that motivated her. That said, more than one garden visitor came to me in some distress to tell me that Saffron was just finishing a late lunch of rabbit in the middle of the front vista - not a pleasant sight as the rear end was usually the last part to be devoured. Despite her poor timing all I could do was smile - very glad that she, at least, was keeping the population down.

There was no way of stopping rabbits getting into the garden. They lived in a network of warrens in the adjoining woodland. When the *Rosa rugosa* hedge was cut to ground level in the 1990s, Philip dug in new netting to try to stop their entry from the copse on the opposite side of the lane. The five bar gate at the bottom of the garden was also netted but to no avail. There was always somewhere they could come through. The rabbits, having finished their dawn feast on the vegetable garden, used to hop down onto the path and across the Stump Garden. When we would see them playing down the garden under the two junipers; Saffron was encouraged to give chase; they would scatter in every direction with no real hope of catching any of them. To my constant dismay they frequently ate the newly emerging herbaceous greenery and stripped bark from low branches but their worst sin of all was to eat the tulip leaves as they emerged in spring.

The garden also became a desirable location for several species of deer. These elegant creatures wandered unafraid during the day. Lying off to ruminate in the long grass in the wilder parts of the garden. In many ways we should have felt privileged that they felt so comfortable in our environment. And maybe, in the early years of gardening, I did see their presence as and honour and didn't minding sharing my plants and trees with them. However as the garden grew in popularity and the need to strive for more perfection for the paying public became more important, they became a foe. They had no fear of us. On one occasion, a red stag with his branched antlers held aloft, wandered down from the top lawn onto the east lawn with a group of smaller deer who I assumed were his family. It was mid morning; he gave the impression that he was taking them on a tour of the choicest parts of the garden. Roses grew on pergolas along the edge of this lawn; the young growth of which was taken regularly by deer. When I returned with my camera they had gone.

Whilst potting in the shed, roe and red deer would wander up through the Goat Wood; I am not sure who was more startled when we came face to face; I suspect it was me because they had moved through with silent stealth. They only bounded away as I let out an exclamation of surprise. The stocky Muntjacs were the most lively and nervy. They regularly alarmed me as they dashed across the lane from the farmer's field and came bouncing over the *Rosa rugosa* hedge as if they had springs attached to their hooves.

All deer are grazers or browsers. Over the years they caused a fair degree of disruption, sometimes on a large scale. One spring they ate the flowers from all the tulips along the Salix Walk just days before we opened for the NGS, leaving nothing but green sentinels. In the early years of the nursery, they carried off their favourite plants and shrubs in the pots, depositing the chewed remains in the top orchard. When the pink and white border had been planted up, they came a few days later and removed many of the specimens from the soil; leaving them strewn across the top arboretum. The lateral growth of the yew hedge, which was just beginning to meld together, was torn apart one morning; the bushes chewed into odd shapes and in some places through to the bark.

More than four hundred tulips were planted in the borders one autumn. The following year the majority were either grazed at ground level as they emerged, or, if allowed to grow, the delicious green buds would be left 'waiting'. Waiting for the deer to eat them. Sometimes, rarely, you would be lucky enough to actually see the flowers open, but the next day, even more frustratingly, you would be left with hundreds of green stalks standing to attention like well regimented soldiers. Some browsed plants are able regenerate for enjoyment later in the year, with slightly shorter growth and possibly fewer flowers but with tulips this is not the case. One of the first joys of spring ended abruptly in a nights' feast. In desperation, the following autumn, an eclectic mix of *Tulipa* 'Queen of the Night' a deep velvety maroon, 'Recreado' a doge-purple with violet-purple flame from the base and 'Negrita' a deep purple, were planted in the square pots either side of the front patio steps. Surely the deer would not enjoy walking on the gravel? Besides sleeping, as we most often did, with our window open there was a strong possibility that we could hear them. But no, every bloom was taken one night. No deterrent seemed effective in any way.

A friend suggested that we put a salt lick and some food in the woodland in the hope of keeping the deer to that area; but we knew they came from all directions. Many of them lived in the copse on the other side of the farm lane. As a deterrent we soaked old rags in creosote, hanging them from posts at various places around the perimeter; but after a couple of heavy rain showers they needed to be redone. I bagged hair cuttings (from my hairdresser friend) in old tights and hung these on the same posts. Once the rain had cleaned the hair a few times, the human scent was eradicated and they too had to be redone. It would have been impossible and far too expensive to fence off the garden. As with most of the foes we learnt to live with them.

We had a certain tolerance towards squirrels; a friend had warned us that we would never be without at least one family in the garden. If you managed to rid the garden of one pair, another pair would move in. As a young adult I remember Gay's anger when she found a neat pile of shucked pea pods in the vegetable garden. At first she thought it might have been the children:

'Would they have left the evidence so neatly stacked?' I asked. She quickly realised that it must have been the squirrels. In my years at Orchards I discovered a similar pile of unripe strawberries stripped from the plants and stashed in the corner of our kitchen garden. I wasn't sure if the squirrels ate them green or whether they were hoping that they might ripen! But there wasn't a strawberry left on any plant.

There was no end to their ingenuity; we were amused at first at the squirrel's antics on the bird feeder. They would spend an age working, nibbling, reworking a nut through the mesh of the feeder until it was small enough for them to steal. When Philip made the nut holder more secure with a slightly finer net, they retaliated by taking the entire holder from the branch - we found it further up the garden taken apart and emptied. We overcame this by purchasing a very superior ceramic bird feeder with a wide roof which overhung the stouter mesh feed holder, with a ceramic base. The squirrels could no longer hold on to any of the slippery parts; and the tiny pieces of nuts on the ground were far too inferior for the squirrels to bother with.

Sadly then became increasingly destructive one year and caused devastation on an enormous scale. This same friend was to tell us that, when you have competing squirrels in your garden, they cause mayhem. The trunk of a beautiful mature copper beech which (Gay had grown from a seed taken from a friend's garden in the locality) was stripped of its bark. Its buttress roots were also decimated, tiny particles of bark littered the ground beneath the canopy. It was this that we had first noticed. We instantly blamed the deer but as we looked up we could see dark rivulets of moisture oozing from the top of the tree down the trunk; the beech was weeping. It was then that we realised that the damage had been caused by the squirrels. They had worked their way along every branch stripping the top layers of bark away. In the weeks that followed they ringed one *Acer* sapling; closer inspection made it difficult to believe that it was an animal who had executed such a neat job.

Another mature gold-leaved *Acer* near the top greenhouses had all the bark stripped from its trunk in an afternoon. It lay around the bole like a thick mulch. I was reduced to tears. *Acers* are a favourite of the squirrel because of the sweet sap-filled layer called phloem tissue, which runs just beneath the bark. If ringed, the tree dies. Damage to the bark of any kind can lead to disease and fungal attack. The *Acer* was cut back to below the squirrel damage and for a while was left as a large shrub rather than a graceful tree. Its fight for survival led it to send a multitude of shoots along its surface roots. As a mature tree it had looked magnificent against a tall, dark green conifer - now it looked dwarfed and out of place.

Moles and their hills never worried me in my early gardening days. Arthur had confirmed that the soil was excellent to use in compost making. The little mounds were collected by the barrow load, wheeled to the greenhouse and mixed into which ever grade of compost was required. The earth was friable and pest free. However once the garden was open to the public the molehills were an unsightly eyesore and their collapsed runs were a hazard which were openly cursed by us both. We no longer collected the soil for compost making; those lazy hazy days of gardening lost forever. Now we used the tractor and trailer; scooping soil up and re-laying in the areas where the turf had subsided into the moles' unused tunnels. It became a major part of the garden's maintenance. We once sought the advice of a mole catcher; I asked many questions of this man and he was honest enough to admit that they could, in fact undoubtedly would, come back on a regular basis and he could give no guarantees for the not insubstantial fee he would want to lay traps. This was yet another foe we learnt to live with; me more graciously than Philip. With such a rich diet of molluscs, other invertebrates and insect larvae - and any damage to plants unintentional - they could almost be considered friends.

Along the entire length of the swathe of grass that divided the wild garden on the northern edge of the plot; golf ball sized holes dotted the grass. As most people wore sensible garden-visiting shoes it wasn't too much of a problem. We never once detected a vole in this area but one visitor told us with great authority that this is what all the holes represented; an enormous city of voles. They enjoy an environment of tender root systems; in this part of the garden there was a wealth of choice.

We had a solitary vole that nested along the sandstone wall behind the house which gave us a great deal of entertainment. He didn't appear to cause any major damage to the abundant ground cover planting of herbaceous or bulbs but we did see him take entire leaves including the stalk from *Geranium versicolor* in particular; carrying it off like a trophy and popping down the largest hole. Whether this was to store for eating or for bedding we didn't know. The vole had other exits along the sandstone wall edging the steps and he would amuse us as he popped out from the planting holes Philip had left uncemented dashing across the steps into another similar hole on the opposite side. In summer we would watch the vole and visiting field mice climb the stems of the *Geranium phaeum* seedlings taking the seed heads in their paws.

Of course most of us dislike anything or anybody who disturbs our sleep. And we often had mice in the attic. We would lie in bed sometimes wondering just what they were up to. They moved imaginary furniture; played games and one definitely had a limp; or so it seemed as it scampered up and over the ceiling joists. That part of the attic was unboarded so to observe closely was almost impossible. Outside they regularly had a feast in the frames and greenhouses where they ate, looted and stored bulbs. Not only did they scrabble in the pots for the newly planted seeds and eat the new growth, they also behaved just as badly in the garden;

where they ate newly planted bulbs or nibbled emerging foliage. After the death of our aged cats the problem escalated.

They stripped bark from a large specimen of *Itea ilicifolia,* a particularly treasured shrub given to me by Rosemary Verey. This mouse did not collect and store, it used the *Itea* as a ready-made larder - the fresh growing stem stripped slowly upwards as it went. When I discovered the ravaged plant in late February whilst trimming back the previous years' flower stems, I noticed a halting in the growth, the dullness that appears on a plant that is suffering, and the change in colour attracted my eye. Parting the branches, the damage was widespread and had obviously been caused over a period of time. Further investigation showed another three feet of stem laid to waste and a few leaf joints tenderly nibbled. I remember cursing mildly and wondering if this was perhaps the same chap who habitually woke me about an hour after I had gone to sleep? Was this the rascal who went across the joists in the attic like an old person with a limp? Who woke me again at 5am on his way out for breakfast? All the wounds were treated with petroleum jelly as a barrier to infection or disease but the *Itea* died.

In my childhood I had held magpies in awe. From the nursery rhyme *'One for sorrow, two for joy...'* a solitary magpie was more frequently seen, usually pulling carrion from the road as you drove towards it. I used to wonder what sorrow would befall me on those days. As an adult I disliked them for their destruction of newly laid eggs or emerging nestlings. Their haughty attitude and strutting manner was a sharp contrast to their beautiful plumage; which from a distance was black and white but on closer inspection (and their arrogance to your presence allowed this) the blackness has a purple-blue glistening lustre and the tail is glossed with green. Of course for them to take the life of young birds or to feast on unhatched eggs was quite natural. I often considered the apparent contradiction of my feelings. The eating of leatherjackets, spiders and other insects by predators felt acceptable to me - I loved the robin that gardened with me and felt glad to see him gobble up wireworms and vine weevil larvae - yet for magpies to kill birds or to take their eggs was not. Yet it is all part of an acknowledged cycle. Magpies have many roles, scavenger, predator and pest destroyer however I found it impossible to like them.

It was with enormous pleasure that Philip and I watched a pair of long-tailed tits make a nest in the middle of a large evergreen *Berberis* bush. We noted the birds daily and felt glad for the protection the nest would have from the prickly host. Philip peeked inside the *Berberis* at the completed ball of lichen, feathers, hair and moss. We waited with anticipation. A few days later we were sad to see that the bush was laden with feathers and scraps of the once neatly constructed nest and on the ground lay pieces of white, purplish-red spotted eggshell.

Philip made nesting boxes and fixed them in numerous places around the garden, on the outbuildings and the side of the house. They were safe havens for our smaller feathered friends. One was placed directly outside our bedroom window. From our bed we could watch the blue-tits coming and going, with nesting material and later with their beaks full of food. On a couple of occasions we witnessed the efforts of the magpie trying to enlarge the hole in an attempt to attack the hatchlings. Philip repaired this damage every time. One morning a magpie flew down and this time successfully scooped out the nestlings. We leapt from bed. Startled, the magpie dropped his prey. Philip hurried downstairs and rescued them all from the border below, before they were taken again. He placed them back inside their house and within days the fledglings were down on the patio outside the kitchen window resting on a giant pot.

A pair of blackbirds loitered at the corner of the house; every now and again they left the veranda as the front door opened. So confident and fearless they appeared to be, it took us sometime before we realised that they were making a nest on the small shelf in front of the airbrick on the wall of the house. Motionless the female sat as we trundled back and forth replenishing barrows of logs for the fire or opening the door to welcome in the sun. With pride we showed off our nest to family and friends; at a respectful distance from the bird. We felt privileged that they felt so confident in our presence. Huge sadness was felt when the fluffy greyish feathers on the gravel warned us of the babies' fate. They had all gone.

Pheasants are handsome foes, especially the male with his burnished chestnut, golden-brown and black markings, glossy dark green head and red face wattling. Many of the males also had the suggestion of a white collar (these I believe are not native) - they were amusing birds to watch with their almost hesitant walk and their slight ducking of the head like an old fashioned comedian. They would crouch slightly, as if to hide, if they heard you coming and only fly off with a great deal noise and wing flapping if they were startled. Their flight appeared a little cumbersome and they would run quite a way before they were airborne. The females had the same mannerisms and, although considered dull in appearance, for me the subtlety of their camouflage colours of light brown and black markings somehow made them more beautiful than the male. You could hear them at night as they went to roost in the trees (with a great fluttering of wings and a cluck to each other). I came across more than one female nesting in the overgrown borders at Orchards, well hidden until I removed the weeds. I felt guilty at having discovered them and on more than one occasion she abandoned the olive-brown clutch of eggs.

The pheasants were not welcomed; so many escaping from the nearby woodland where they were raised for the seasonal shoot, that they became a nuisance in the garden. They had more sense than to remain in the woodland once grown, preferring the abundant greenness of our garden and the cover it afforded to the prepared feed given by their keeper. Huge patches of foliage disappeared beneath the pecking of thirty or forty of them at a time. They also enjoyed digging and prodding for invertebrates and devouring the fallen fruit in the orchards. The guys on the shoot asked more than once to beat across the garden. I wouldn't allow this, as by October some of the early daffodils could be showing their leaves - or at least that was my excuse. Much as I loathed the pheasants intrusion, I felt very smug on the Shooting Days when they moved rapidly back into the garden away from the guns and the beaters. It warmed my heart on those occasions that they found shelter and felt safe at Orchards. One damp autumnal day, more than twenty lady pheasants spent the morning on the back patio just waiting for the local pub to call the guys away!

Ground Elder was one of the many pernicious weeds that I inherited when I moved to Orchards. It was there in my childhood and fifty years later it was still with me. Three different strategies helped; one was to mulch; as densely as my pocket could afford, with mushroom compost. The second, when beaten yet again by the flourishing growth, was to rip it out in handfuls. Occasionally, it would come out with long white surface roots intact - not unlike bindweed - growing away happily in the newly mulched layer. The third, not as acceptable in many people's opinion but something that experience dictated was necessary; was to weed kill as soon as new growth appeared. Forget the 'right' time of year, length of day etc. Cover any growth from nearby herbaceous plants with upturned flowerpots and water - sorry weed kill - the fresh new elder leaves that in most places were already growing higher than neighbouring plants. As long as there was no rain for at least an hour - that was one instruction I did adhere to - the liquid would set. One 'qualified' colleague tore me off a strip for dealing with this too early in the season, but I had the advantage over a qualification - experience. Later in the year she had to admit that she had 'missed the optimum moment' in her own garden! Mark you; used earlier in the season it took much longer to kill, but the growth was halted. This then allowed the abundant planting of the hardy perennials to come through.

Bryonia dioica - Sweet briony - was almost impossible to eradicate. It sent up brownish leafless stems which would wave around until they found a bush to lean on, the coiled tendrils winding their way through, scrambling to the top, covering the host with drooping racemes of greenish-white flowers in the male and lateral clusters in the female. By the time the bright palmate leaves had unfurled it could not be sprayed with weedkiller, unless I had taken time to remove it and deal with it on the ground. It would have been too time consuming to do this or to 'spot weed' - wearing a rubber glove on one hand and painting with a stencil brush directly onto the leaf. It was time I could ill afford to spend on such a thankless task and, truth be told I did have a secret admiration for the plant. Bees and small insects used it for pollination and the autumn berries which turned from green to scarlet when ripe, were a joy to see.

It was only with a shadow of guilt that I cursed our native bindweed with its brilliant white trumpets. To be honest I admired its ability to twist its way up large shrubs and roses before I had noticed it. I smiled at the flowers basking in the sun. It is known by several other names - Devil's Guts, Bearbind, and Hell Weed. All were very apt names for a problematic weed; which was never completely eradicated from the garden. It was easier to deal with than *Bryonia dioica.* In the worst affected areas bamboo stakes were inserted where

233

the new shoots emerged; they would twine around the canes, which were then laid on the soil and sprayed with a systemic weedkiller. I spent an entire day hand weeding roots in an area I knew to be overrun. I took barrow loads of them to the bonfire to be burnt. Then, satisfied that I had removed every tiny piece of root because even the minutest piece would regrow - I placed the selected herbaceous plants in their pots and dug holes with a spade. One spit down a spaghetti junction of roots lay matted and at this point I admitted defeat. I did return to this area often through the year and sprayed as soon as I detected the new shoots; and later in the season when deadheading or cutting back I would pull long surface stems already trying to root at the leaf axils. At the front of the border I did enjoy the few stems that escaped and scrambled through the nearby shrubs, entwined with the dark purple of *Clematis* 'Lady Betty Balfour' and flowered pure white trumpets.

With damper autumns and milder winters many of the annual ephemeral weeds continued to grow, flower and seed. Chickweed was the most prolific, closely followed by cleavers or stickywilly - *Galium aparine*. Tiny seedlings were seen as early as November; another reason why the garden could never be put to bed. Chickweed can mature and set its first seed within five weeks. As with all garden weeds it is prudent to learn the cotyledonary stage of growth; they can then be picked out before they become a problem. Cleavers are distributed around the garden as the hooked seeds attach to your clothing or the fur of passing animals. We found it in massed tangles in the wild garden; the hens loved it and quickly trod down and separated the piles that we gave them. We never dealt with this weed without our legs and arms being covered; on unclothed flesh the tiny hooks would leave us with a nasty rash.

Some weeds seemed fitting to the woodland garden at Orchards - I couldn't completely do away with a small clump of lesser celandine that grew in the shade near the house. Its early glossy bright yellow flowers were always appreciated - it did however get a dose of weedkiller around the edges when the ground elder in the border was being sprayed. Nearby a small clump of coltsfoot was also allowed to flower but not seed. Creeping buttercup, *Runuculus repens* was welcome in the apple-tree meadow and in the orchards, but having found its way into the stock in the top nursery, it became a real problem. The stoloniferous stems rooted at every leaf node, even on the soil-less surface of the ground cover. It climbed up and over the pots establishing itself at every opportunity, the fibrous roots taking over from its host plant in the pot.

I know that *Petasites japonicus* is not a weed; it is a Japanese native, but in the pond garden at Orchards it behaved very badly and spread from its designated area, off under the fence and through the adjoining woodland. Our nearest neighbours must have cursed us. In the bareness of winter and early spring you forgot what a thug it really was. A member of the *Asteraceae* family its crown of whitish-yellow flowers with a ruff of green was a welcome sight; the late spring growth of its *Gunnera*-like leaves engulfed any other nearby plants. It is described in books as clump-forming with a maximum spread of five feet - this was not the case in my garden. It ran in every direction becoming more thug-like each year. The pond garden was situated at the most southerly part of the grounds; by the time any systemic weedkilling would have been possible, the other borders received all the attention. It was never open to the public for this reason. We never quite managed to keep this area under any kind of control. It was loved by others though - on two occasions I caught people digging out this plant without our permission.

Gay had introduced 'Mind Your Own Business', *Soleirolia soleirolii* as a houseplant. Somehow it found its way into Arthur's greenhouse and became a real nuisance; the slim lax stems root as they run and very quickly a carpet of tiny leaves covered the soil. I would see it for sale at garden shows, a neat hummock of tiny leaves. Had I not known its true habit once set free, I would have been enticed to buy a pot. I was tempted to leave a note nearby 'Buy with caution'. I saw it used to great effect in a small suburban garden where it was used in place of grass. It was allowed to run over rocks, cascade down garden steps and clothe the landscape. If frosted in the winter, it recovered in the spring. All that was needed, if it became invasive, was a sharp pair of scissors.

I was influenced by a very persuasive volunteer to leave seed heads for the birds; it was a costly mistake in time at least. A giant of an *Echinops* (given to me by a friend) which was tucked into the corner of the Yew border grew to at least seven feet in height. The tits who fed off it were a pleasure to watch, but the seedlings were found yards away in other borders where they were not wanted. They send down the longest taproot, for the pair of innocent green leaves above ground; making them very difficult to remove. Seven years later we still found seedlings in the nearby borders, despite the fact that the offending *Echinops* had been relegated to the pond garden.

Honey fungus was a lethal fungus approaching with the stealth of a serial killer; often doing most of its damage before we were even aware of its presence. It claimed as one of its victims, a huge specimen sweet chestnut, bursting with new spring leaves. One week later half of the tree began to fail. The foliage stopped growing, becoming listless and shrivelled. Honey fungus had hit only one side of the root system. This is the unpredictable way of this fungus; which spreads its rhizomorphs through the soil; existing as a parasite feeding on the tree roots. Honey fungus is not one specific fungus; it is the common name for several species of fungi in the genus *Armillaria*. Often at Orchards we would chat about the toadstools which would appear in the woodlands and discuss as to whether it was honey fungus or not. But even within their own species they can have different habits and colouring - the only thing common amongst them all, is the white 'collar' beneath the gills. The conclusive symptom to indicate honey fungus is the layer of white mycelium which is present beneath the bark of the tree; with a strong smell of mushroom. A visitor to the garden declared that she could 'sniff it out'.

An ancient Chinese poplar, grafted onto other rootstock, suffered and fought for years against honey fungus. Its trunk became almost hollow, the inside wet and sappy but every year it hung its extraordinary large catkins in the spring, produced large leaves and later fluffy white seed heads. We didn't have the heart to remove it. Then one spring; its slow growing neighbour *Picea breweriana* turned brown overnight. The only shrubs in the garden that seemed to be honey fungus-proof were *Rhododendron, Azalea* and *Camellia*. In areas where we knew it was rife, these survived unscathed. The toadstools appeared in autumn in large clusters beneath affected trees and shrubs, but also occasionally in the middle of the grass where the rhizomorphs were present.

Three old silver birches grew in the top northwest corner of the garden. One showed identical signs of suffering to the sweet chestnut. Arthur methodically removed the lower branches, dug a trench around the root plate and with the help of an iron plate levered with an iron bar, gradually pushing the tree over; cutting way any stubborn roots as he went. He liked this kind of gardening, sometimes taking several days to achieve his purpose. It was only as a last resort that you could have persuaded him to get a tree surgeon in to fell it. The hurricane of 1987 swept its way through the garden leaving the exposed birch still standing and its two healthy neighbours on the ground! We learnt to live with nature and all it had to offer.

Saffron guarding the stump

Part Three

Serendipity

I could describe the eleven years that followed Arthur's death as a rollercoaster but it wouldn't be accurate because there were far more ups than downs. It was more like a wild water ride. A wave of enthusiasm took us though the sixteen months after his passing; working as hard as I ever had, to make the garden acceptable to the National Gardens Scheme. We were carried along on a rush of eagerness following the first open weekend. Grass Roots, a Meridian Television programme, featured the garden and a local newspaper, the Argus printed a piece to advertise the garden's first opening.

A new sweet pea was introduced in 1994 by Unwin seeds. A competition was held in Gardeners' World Magazine inviting readers to name a new sweet pea to celebrate Unwin's ninetieth anniversary. I entered - suggesting that as Arthur had reached his ninetieth birthday six weeks before his death - maybe that would be an appropriate opportunity to mark both occasions. It was chosen. Described as having, *'bold, fragrant blooms with a white background, heavily flushed with lavender'*, it is still on sale today. It was raised by Mr

R W Francis. We were invited to the Gardeners' World Live Show held at Birmingham, where I was presented with a sweet pea vase inscribed with Arthur's name.

Philip and I had worked together in the garden since 1989 with no thought then of opening the garden to the public. I was propagating furiously with a plan to rejuvenate the garden and to sell at the local farm shop, garden shows and occasionally at the garden gate. Maybe if Arthur had lived a few more years the garden would never have been opened. Although he would have been proud of our improvements, he was reluctant to have many people see his garden. During his lifetime, only a chosen few had ever had a personal guided tour. He'd made a pact with his colleague Robin Lane Fox that they would not see each others gardens whilst they worked together.

Robin joined Arthur at the Financial Times as their mid-week gardening contributor in 1970. There was no collaboration on the content of each other's weekly articles, yet they never clashed about what they wrote. The pact not to visit each other's gardens was upheld. It was not until after Arthur's death that Robin came to Orchards to interview me for his article in *Gardens Illustrated* September 2001. A further article appeared in the Weekend Financial Times section in 4-5 May 2002. He was, and still is, Arthur's most stalwart champion. In an article titled *'Our Own Hardy Perennial'* in the Financial Times House & Home section 5 September 2010; he wrote about him again. It drew attention to the fact that Arthur gets a mention in his new book *'Thoughtful Gardening: Great Plants, Great Gardens, Great Gardeners'*, published in 2010. Since Arthur's death, Robin has referred to him often in his articles and still draws information and guidance from his books describing the *Amateur Gardening Pocket Guide* as his 'practical bible'.

The late Kathleen Hudson, an acquaintance of Arthur's, confided in me that she had walked the garden several times with Arthur after Gay had died; and although appreciative of all the magnificent trees and shrubs had noticed how neglected it had become. 'Jim' as she was known, (I never learnt why), was a very special lady who lived nearby and became a good friend to us from my early nursery days. She would bring her friends and family to both the nursery and the garden; often on a day of closure. She became a great supporter of our project. The best advice she gave me was *'to give the garden at least half an hours' work a day.'* This could include just browsing seed or bulb catalogues or gazing from the window on a rainy day deciding how to improve a border. She had made a garden of her own in her fifties; simplifying it in later life as her hips became increasingly immobile. We chatted about the different ways one learnt to cope with weeding as our arthritis became more troublesome. *'There is always a solution or a strong man nearby,'* she would say with a broad grin. Jim was welcoming to people from all walks of life and any age. She painted every day. If you took her lilies for her birthday they would be remembered on canvas before they faded. She gave us one of her oil paintings of white camellias as a wedding present and we bought a further oil painting of blue gentians from her at a later date.

§

During my time at Orchards I undid much that Arthur had done over the previous years. As he'd grown older, he had reduced the number of herbaceous borders; planting more shrubs in their place or returning areas back to grass. I increased our workload with each month that went by as my passion for perennials grew. Anyone who knew me well knew that my favourite plants were hardy *Geraniums*, although it was also true

246

that first time visitors to the garden and nursery very quickly realised my addiction too. It is one of the plants that Rosemary Verey told me to specialise in; however as so many of the species were ideal for a woodland garden I would have grown them anyway.

Those same people also knew that I would purchase a plant for its foliage alone; any flower being a bonus. *Geranium phaeum* 'Samobor' was a good example; each lobe of the large leaves strikingly marked dark brown. The autumn colours of yellow, red and ochre on *Geranium wlassovianum* leaves, grown on the shady borders outside the cabin, were far superior to the prettily marked pale bluish-purple flowers borne in summer or the bronze of the new spring growth. The variegated cultivar of *Geranium phaeum* 'Margaret Wilson', described by David Hibberd as *'one of the best variegated geraniums with its leaves evenly marbled creamy white'*, was a choice plant, lighting up many shady corners. The golden-yellow foliage of *Geranium* 'Ann Folkard' or *G.* 'Blue Sunrise' was a great addition to the spring garden; when the neat mounds of so many of the *Geraniums* exude an innocence soon lost in the breathtaking luxuriance of summer growth. The true beauty of many of them is in their flowers; for the main

247

part a simple single bowl or saucer-shape reminiscent of a wild rose. Many others are single trumpet-shaped, a few are double as in *Geranium pratense* 'Plenum Caeruleum' or with a strange twisted effect to the petals as in *Geranium* x *oxonianum* f. *thurstonianum*. In sharp contrast to the simplicity of the flower shape is the veining and dramatic contrasting colours in the different flowers. I wish now I'd had more time to either photograph these striking veins more closely or better still time to paint them. If you have grown hardy *Geraniums* for any length of time you will know that they are very useful, versatile, accommodating plants. There are species for every conceivable garden situation. Many people know that they can climb up through shrubs but against a wall was a new and interesting idea.

The sight of a *Geranium* x *oxonianum* cultivar gazing at me from the top of the trellis on the north wall of the house used to make me smile. Very much better I thought to grow like that, than the matted thatch neglected *G.* x *oxonianum* cultivars can make. I had long wondered about the use of hardy *Geraniums* as climbers. I had grown *G. procurrens* for many years and knew that it could travel five to six feet on its trailing stems, rooting at every leaf axil if it touched the ground making an untidy but delightful carpet throughout the flower borders. These stems died back in the winter leaving only the basal growths to flower the following year. On a visit to Barnsley House, I saw it growing against the stone wall, woven between an unnamed small-flowered clematis. What a delight to be able to admire it at eye level. The only drawback for the propagator would be the lack of 'free' rooted layers.

§

Orchards became so much more than our home, so much more that just a garden. It was my daughter Sorcha who declared it *'a patch of heaven'*. As we developed structure in the hard landscaping and planting, the pretty wooden house that Gay and Arthur had built, nestled beautifully within the established surroundings. The cedar walls had matured to a deep mole grey; the perfect foil for climbing plants. Gay and Arthur had grown several climbers against the walls; I added a few dozen more. An ancient wisteria planted on the south-west corner of the original part of the house, completed in 1938, snuggled against the veranda and trailed above and beneath the lounge windows of the 1949 extension. A couple of stems had layered themselves and scrambled up a wire support; these had aged to a thick trunk, the lateral growth billowed from the corner of the house. New stems were guided along the west elevation of the house towards a *Clematis armandii* planted years before. It didn't flourish on this wall but neither did it die. Whether the *Phygelius* x *rectus* 'African Queen' with its suckering habit was too much competition, or the heat from the chimney which ran up the middle of this wall was too intense, I'm not sure. On the north wall a *Lonicera* flowered happily in poor soil and little sun, barely tied into the wire stretched the length of the wall. The east wall was host to *Clematis montana* 'Elizabeth' on the north corner and *Chaenomeles speciosa* 'Moerloosei' on the southern corner. The latter was clipped hard back against the wall; its tangled spiny branches best contained. Clusters of pink buds flowered directly from the bare stems, opening to white blushed pink, or flushed deep pink and fading to white with age; before the glossy leaves emerged. I often felt a tinge of guilt at the large greenish-yellow fruits which clung within the twisted branches or fell to the ground. These could have been used for preserves and jelly or gently poached but I never made the time to do so. Far more plants are happy on north facing walls than is realised. One frequently thinks of plants thriving better in warm, sunny, sheltered positions. Many years previously whilst trying to deal with the narrow border on the north of the house, books and then catalogues were referred to.

North wall in 2004 - *Hydrangea petiolaris* **to the left of the door**

This border - after several layers of clay was removed and replaced with barrow loads of grit and mole hills - was planted up with roses, clematis and ground cover plants. The old honeysuckle from Gay and Arthur's day was tied onto a new narrow trellis; the rose and the honeysuckle were allowed to climb to the top of this and then they were cut off, tied in or both. On the sunniest corner of this north facing border, I planted *Clematis* 'Nelly Moser' with soft pink flowers marked with a darker pink bar down each petal, only the first two feet was tied to canes, any new growths were then flung onto an adjacent *Camellia*.

Pulmonaria saccharata seeded prolifically, the pretty blue and pink flowers with their spotted leaves a constant; responding well to being cutback several times a year. An original clump of white hellebore seeded profusely in the annual mulch of mushroom compost. *Filipendula ulmaria* 'Aurea' enjoyed either the dampness or the shade and the mulch in summer. One of the newly planted *Clematis* was lost when poked into the darkest corner of the trellis - probably eaten by snails or slugs. *Rosa* 'Mrs Herbert Stevens', a shapely rose with a sweet scent took a couple of years to settle. It was tied along the length of trellis and gave more flowers in successive years. In slightly less sun was *Clematis* 'Dorothy Walton', flowering later than *C.* 'Nelly Moser', although sometimes late large blossoms of this blended well with the dullish-lilac of *C.* 'Dorothy Walton', and when they did the combination of the two was stunning. The latter had particularly lovely seedpods. The only other herbaceous planting in this little border was pink Japanese anemone and *Luzula nivea.*

Feedback from our garden visitors confirmed that *Clematis* was still underrated - an unpruned one was once described by the late Christopher Lloyd as a *'disembowelled mattress.'* Many gardeners were put off buying more *Clematis* by the loss of a probably immature specimen being planted in their garden. In the late 1990s low-priced but young plants, whose foliage was too soft, could be snapped up at some garden outlets; lack of knowledge led to a large number dying before they became established. Some of my nursery visitors would eye my stock with suspicion. None of my plants were sold until they had matured to fill two litre pots. More often than not, those that I had bought for the garden, needed to be grown on until they did the same before I would plant them out. Incorrect planting of *Clematis*, for the new or nervous gardener, drew the same emotions as pruning. I was in my early twenties when non-gardening friends reflected on my zealous approach to pruning, claiming that the plants quivered noticeably whenever I walked with secateurs or loppers along the paths.

But back to *Clematis*; unlike the rules which apply to so many plants, they can be buried even deeper than they come out of the pot. Those lifeless-looking twiggy stems - if you were lucky enough to have more than one - would develop additional roots quite readily. If you have ever potted on internodal cuttings they, in some cases, have roots that appear not only at the leaf joint but often further down the stem. All wall plants should be placed at least two feet away from the wall, I was told, unless you are prepared to water. I felt immense gratitude to my thirty plus climbers and shrubs around the walls of the house, for behaving so well and growing on so healthily, despite the neglect and 'incorrect' planting.

One source of great pride to me was the stamina of *Clematis armandii* 'Snowdrift', planted in front of the south facing guest room window, on the eastern side. It had been trained along the entire length of the veranda and around the corner to flower with the existing wisteria on the western side. It had also been encouraged towards the east wall to flower on the extensive trellis that Philip built to accommodate the multitude of plants growing there. It was excellent value for money and certainly aptly named. The only downside was that once mature, the older evergreen leaves began to die-off. Unlike with deciduous clematis (where you may be tempted to remove entire stems to tidy); the job is much more painstaking. It wouldn't have been the last time that, despite having diligently worked along the climber removing only brown leaves, a momentary lack of concentration led to me cutting a dead looking stem, only to discover it held perfectly good growth; wasting hours of careful work, tying in, and cutting back new growth etc. This was a mistake I first made in my late twenties and frustratingly continued to make years later. On a positive note, it was a glorious sight in flower; opening its waxy, white blossoms one at a time with swollen creamy buds behind - its heady almond scent filling the bedroom at night. Earlier in the year the new bronze leaves would add a touch of glamour, long before the blossoms opened. We would watch the buds swelling, eagerly anticipating their blooms and, quite often in a warm spring, the first flowers had burst open without us even noticing.

Clematis rehderiana clambered through the wisteria and dripped small yellow cowslip-scented bells in autumn. I loved it, buying it for its coarse nettle-like leaves and the delicate unassuming flower, not knowing then its delightful fragrance. Another favourite was *Clematis* 'My Angel' with delicate greyish-green foliage and tiny orange-peel flowers. Despite its fragile appearance it managed to scramble to the bedroom windows, with the added attraction of flowering on its journey covering the entire wall with blooms.

All of these permanent wall plants were further adorned through the summer months, by annual climbers. *Ipomoea* was one that we used in great numbers. Seed discovered in Arthur's cupboard was at least ten years old yet these germinated and flowered fuchsia pink trumpets. Sadly none of these set any seed but other colours, both purchased and donated, gave an eclectic mix of deepest purple, blue and sky-blue - some striped, some not. On the east wall they made large heart-shaped leaves with fewer flowers; against a sunny wall their foliage was smaller but far more floriferous. We also planted them in hanging baskets which had been lined with sphagnum moss from the garden. A circle cut from an old compost bag was then laid on top of the moss, creating a liner to retain water and filled with compost. Cuts were made in the plastic at intervals around the basket; the *Ipomoea* was pushed through the holes around the edges and in the middle. A second hanging basket was wired upside down to the one beneath. The planted baskets were then hung from the frame in my new greenhouse; sheltered from excessive cold or rain. As the *Ipomoea* developed and sent out early tendrils, the flexible shoots were guided in and out of the holes just to give a bare covering of the structure, then it was left to its own devices. This was not for the tidy minded, as by late June it was a disorderly jumble of heart-shaped leaves and trumpet flowers. Another favourite hanging basket was the 'nasturtium basket' made in the same way with a mix of orange, yellow and yellow-streaked orange flowers. One year I planted up a series of salad hanging baskets containing lettuce, salad leaves, rocket, nasturtium, chives and baby hanging tomatoes - for a customer. They were a great success as their pet rabbit (given free range of their garden) could no longer devour the summer crop.

With the house already dressed, the climbers and wall shrubs became natural supports for the *Geraniums* to climb through. I experimented with a number of this genus as climbers. *Geranium wallichianum* 'Buxton's Variety' with pretty marbled foliage and charming blue saucer-shaped flowers with a white eye, fine magenta veins and a pinkish-blue reverse. *G. w.* RBGE form; (the RBGE stands for Royal Botanic Garden of Edinburgh) which I preferred; the flowers were not dissimilar in shape but the petals were more separate, with a wider, lighter blue edged petal, white centre and stronger magenta veins. The longer dark stamens gave a more dramatic effect, whilst the flowers had a light bluish-pink reverse. *G.* 'Nora Bremner' - which has *G. w* 'Buxton's Variety' as one of its parents was another climbing experiment. The flowers were larger, similar in colour but with a broader band of blue, a white centre and very fine magenta veining, the petals more separate giving an open starry effect. All of these needed a cool root run, in moist but well drained soil.

I particularly liked the trailing stems of beautiful rounded foliage, which carried the white, red-veined flowers of *G* 'Coombland White'; the roots of which required not only good drainage but also light shade. A cross between *G. procurrens* and *G. lambertii*; *G.* 'Salome' had a mound of golden-yellow leaves. The long scrambling stems carried striking palest mauve flowers with a deep purple central eye and strongly marked veins. *G.* 'Joy' - an offspring of *G. lambertii* -

was a pretty, almost evergreen cultivar, with marbled, soft greyish-green foliage and pale pink flowers prominently marked with darker mauve veins.

G. riversleaianum 'Mavis Simpson' delighted me with its clear pink flowers glossed with a silvery sheen above neat mounding grey-green foliage. It dislikes winter wet, so would be ideal for a sunny position or near a wall, thus remaining dry. *G. r.* 'Russell Prichard' is similar to the above but with light magenta flowers. *G.* 'Anne Folkard' and *G.* 'Ann Thomson' are comparable in appearance; both have wonderful gold foliage in the spring, changing to bright green for the rest of the year. Strong magenta flowers with a black eye give a startling contrast. The latter is slightly more compact with a less intense flower colour. They both prefer a sunny position. It was always a challenge to find plants to liven up the climbers on the house. In some cases the lax stems needed a little direction before they began their ascent.

§

The kitchen garden added to the summer workload. I could never quite match the variety or number of vegetables grown by Arthur and Gay. The wealth of their harvest was diverse, giving pickings of greens almost all year round. Brussels sprout tops were eaten long before they had become fashionable to buy in supermarkets. French, runner, and broad beans, peas, carrots, parsnips beetroots turnips, marrows, potatoes - first early, early and main crop - onions, lettuce, spinach, cabbages, curly kale, cauliflower and broccoli were grown.

My first kitchen garden was much more modest and colourful. Rainbow chard was my favourite, glistening stems of ruby-red, yellow and orange. Their young leaves could be eaten in salad, the older ones used in place of spinach and the stems steamed or stir-fried. It was a pleasure to eat our own crops but sometimes the weeks of cultivation could be ruined in moments. I grew blocks of sweetcorn one year to find them, early one morning, ploughed and stripped by the deer. An old fashioned maroon runner bean, given to me by an elderly friend of Arthur's, gave added interest; long before other red vegetables became trendy. When I was cooking them, the children would be fascinated by the colour of the reddish water and the now dull green bean.

The cabbage I grew in the newly planted kitchen garden came under close scrutiny when the television

programme Grass Roots came to the garden with Pippa Greenwood. Prior to filming, I had been asked to leave any pests for their visit. Pippa was still working for the Royal Horticultural Society in plant pathology, so the aphids on my cabbages were a good example. Attention was also drawn to my lupin aphids, the leafhoppers on a bank of *Rhododendron ponticum*, and to the mildew on *Rosa* 'Excelsa'.

Many visitors said, after the programme was shown on television, that the slot made me look ill-informed and felt it hadn't done my reputation any good. I remember Pippa having reservations about concentrating on the pests too intently; the programme was after all meant to be about the garden at Orchards opening to the public for charity. In truth I knew the answers to all the problems and pests, although I didn't express this on film, as this was television and it was publicity for the garden. Many others said it made them feel comfortable in the knowledge I had the same issues as them. Pippa returned in 1995 to 'formally open' the garden at the beginning of the Red Cross Garden Open year. I was presented with a pot of the Humanity rose, especially bred for the Red Cross to mark their 125th Anniversary by Harkness Roses.

Unlike Arthur, who'd had a thorough 'apprenticeship', spending eleven years working in different nurseries; specialising in a wide range of plants; I had no formal training. Some would no doubt argue that being the daughter of such a famous man should have given me the best 'apprenticeship' but that would be naïve and misguided. I did learn from both Gay and Arthur, but not as much as many might have thought. Some would probably have assumed that (besides the environment in which I had the good fortune to grow up) it was likely in my genes. But not everyone knew that I was adopted. Personally I knew the truth of the matter. I was not qualified and had never been ashamed to admit if I didn't know something; always eager to absorb information and advice from others or to be pointed in the right direction. I wanted people to come to the garden to see what we were doing; and to return the following season to see what we had achieved. Many did; for many years. For us the garden was always 'work-in-progress'. With the limitations that governed us we could not possibly have had the garden in pristine order waiting for its public. Nor would we have wanted it to be immaculate anyway. It has to be said however, that

262

Philip would have preferred a more orderly way of planting than he had to live with; especially on the days when it had rained heavily bringing the herbaceous growth spilling over the pathway so that he had to hop and jump along it to make his way to the house.

Given the constraints on my time, my interest moved to perennial vegetables. For me this was defined as growing for more than two years; sometimes longer but easily renewed with the many seedlings that would self-seed. We bought from several specialist nurseries; Iden Croft Herbs in Staplehurst, Kent was our preferred choice. They hold NCCPG National collections of *Mentha*, *Origanum* and *Nepeta* (spp). The national collections are on display just outside the old walled garden. A series of beautiful gardens, which are open to the public, display their herbs and perennials.

The kitchen garden took several guises until I separated the herbs from the vegetables. The new Herb Garden with its boxwood parterres was planted with blocks of herbs and perennial vegetables. Among the plants we bought, and made extensive use of, was French Sorrel - *Rumex scutatus* - its thick green, shield leaves have a taste comparable to a green apple. We also grew *Rumex acetosa* - the broad leaf sorrel - As

263

with French Sorrel, we used the young leaves in salads; the older leaves could be made into soup. Good King Henry - *Chenopodium bonus-henricus* - was another welcome addition. It is thought to have been introduced by the Romans and is often found growing on verges and wasteland. It has a myriad of uses, young leaves for salads, older ones cooked like spinach. When the flower buds begin to show on the young emerging shoots, they can be picked, boiled or steamed and served with butter. Lovage - *Levisticum officinale* - was a favourite; the entire plant can be utilised for culinary purposes. It has an aromatic fragrance of celery and angelica. The young leaves alone are rather pungent but when mixed with other leaves it makes an interesting and flavoursome salad. I loved the fern-like appearance of *Myrrhis odorata*. The white, scented flesh of the thick brown taproot can be cooked as a root vegetable or used raw in salad. The leaves can be added to soups and stews or to omelettes. Seed was given to me - by an elderly garden visitor whose family had grown the Welsh onion - *Allium fistulosum* - for generations. *'All kitchen gardens must have it.'* she said. The bulbs and the leaves can be eaten raw or cooked, the fresh flowers sprinkled on a salad.

Aloysia triphylla - lemon verbena - sheltered on the veranda; wrapped against frost in the winter months. In the summer months it was moved to the gravel terrace where the warmth of the sun lifted the lemony fragrance from the highly scented leaves. It has many culinary uses, in drinks, jams and jellies but I liked just to brush past and rub one of the leaves. The long purple flower spikes of *Agastache foeniculum* - anise hyssop - made an attractive and useful addition; their aniseed-scented leaves used in salads. *Allium schoenoprasum* - the common chive - was used decoratively as edging for the borders in the kitchen garden. To my mind it is essential to have a good crop of this plant. It takes a few weeks for the stems, trimmed for culinary uses to regenerate. If left uncut an attractive edging of spiky leaves and small purple globe flowers remains. These globes can be pulled apart and the flowers added to salads or summer drinks.

My *Angelica* plant was relegated to the long back border - it made a magnificent statuesque statement - strongly branched and covered with large umbels of greenish flowers. Philip hated it with a passion. I can still see the delight on his face when it was finally removed, flung in the trailer and carted off to the bonfire. I could have sworn I heard him mutter, *'At last'*. In the late 1970s I grew a cutting from a large bay tree which leant against the stone wall of a friend's house. It remained on the veranda; I was never certain of its hardiness. Thirty years later it was repotted and placed outside the kitchen window. It was possibly the most frequently used herb. One or two leaves were used in any stock, stew or casserole or a sprig was taken as an essential part of a bouquet garni. *Melissa officinalis* was another present from a gardening colleague. It spread like a weed if not deadheaded but was easily pulled. I loved it for its lemon-scented foliage which we used in stuffing, summer drinks and sparingly in salads. Gay had grown the softly textured apple mint near the garden gate and there it remained; in my opinion it made the best mint sauce. I grew other mints, not so much for their different flavours but for their different coloured leaves. *Mentha* x *piperita* has oval, toothed foliage which is strongly scented peppermint and is said to aid digestion. Pineapple mint; *Mentha suaveolens* 'Variegata' is as soft in texture as apple mint with attractive green and cream variegated foliage.

Other borders in the kitchen garden were edged with *Origanum vulgare* 'Aureum', a delightful luminous plant, shining most golden-yellow in full sun. The tiny oval leaves were used in salads; the tiny pink flowers in summer drew many pollinators. I was told many years previously that feverfew - *Tanacetum parthenium* - would alleviate migraines. Just the musty smell of its leaves left me glad that I didn't suffer from them. Weedy by nature, the gold-leaved specimen was allowed to stay. However, planting *Tanacetum vulgare* - Tansy - directly in the ground was a mistake. Reputed to be a good fly repellent, as well as being used for culinary and medical purposes, with me it was too invasive. It weaved its way in and out of the neat box squares erupting from the earth, even pushing the new box plants from the ground. Hoverflies in particular loved the yellow umbels of the bronze fennel planted in profusion; we hardly ever used this herb but I loved the colour and softness of its foliage; the aniseed fragrance as you weeded nearby and the obvious magnetic pull for the numerous insects in the garden. One border of the kitchen garden contained purple leaved sage. We grew far too much for our needs; nevertheless it made a bold planting statement and a constant food source for

267

the pollinating insects. A selection of low growing thymes was planted in tiny pockets in the steps beneath the front patio steps. This developed into a lovely carpet which when walked on, emitted lemony fragrances. Many of the thymes are lemon-scented but the foliage is varied and interesting. *Thymus citriodorus* has small dark green leaves, while the cultivar, *T. c.* 'Silver Queen' has small silver variegated leaves and *T. c.* 'Doone Valley is variegated yellow and green. I derived so much pleasure from the kitchen garden that I decided that if I ever had only a small patch to look after it would be planted up with fruit, vegetables and herbs only.

§

As my gardening years evolved; I needed to stand still, listen, wait and watch. I needed just to enjoy. The small birds, waiting to feed in the *Magnolia tripetala,* entranced us every time. However busy, we would stop to observe, concentration lapsed any conversation. We smiled at the sight of two coal tits not willing to share the recently replenished tube of peanuts and at the small family of long-tailed tits (these are my favourite birds), the fluffiest ball of down with minute black-bead eyes and beak, flitting ever nearer to share the tube; one flutter of wings from the resident birds sends them scattering further up the tree. This *Magnolia* - grown by Gay from seed given to her by one of her students - would be sprinkled with small birds; moving from branch to branch waiting their turn to feed. The bullies got the most - as in life. The nuthatches used to take the longest time; pecking upside down chiselling away until the reduced (but still intact) nut was finally removed to be consumed elsewhere. An occasional tree creeper would be seen, well camouflaged against the trunk of the tree, creeping with stealth towards the nuts.

The robin would sit patiently, perched on a branch nearby, observing. When enough debris had fallen from the greedy activities above; it would drop to the ground and clear the paving of crumbs. The pretty marsh tits and dunnocks were content to do this too. The added delight for us was to see the lesser spotted woodpecker, he had to wrap himself around the tube in order to peck the nuts within, his red pantaloons on show to the world. One spring he returned accompanied by a youngster, who was even more nervous than the parent, staying high in the *Magnolia* whilst he diligently chopped away, eventually forcing out a nut which he then took it to the fledgling to feed

269

on. Occasionally a linnet or siskin would join in, as did chaffinches, green and gold finches, wrens and goldcrests - all brief visitors to the ground.

Two thrushes used to patrol the yew hedge, darting in and out; this same action was repeated under the shrubs as well; almost running to find a stone or a step to break open their quarry. The blackbirds habitually made the most mess, thrashing the newly mulched borders back over the paths or the grass in their hunt for worms or grubs. The sight of a blackbird and a thrush pulling worms from the Yew border should have been captured on camera; a moment locked in time. The thrush in particular, her feet almost jammed against the soil, pulling and straining to extract a worm from beneath the mulch. I sometimes wondered how the worm felt during this tussle.

So confident were most of the birds in the garden that, if they saw us, they often just turned away a little as if preparing for flight - but then remained. I felt it was only young robins that didn't like us to look at them. Many of the robins in the garden would sit close by and chatter to us, coming closer when we mimicked their sound. One year we were inundated with vine weevil grubs. I collected them in a little saucer for my hens;

and the moment I turned away, a robin was down to eat them. Over a number of days the robin came, as the grubs were placed in the saucer, just like a kitten would lap milk. A few days later, he had become so accustomed to this ritual that he fluttered like a humming bird feeding directly from my hand.

A pair of ringed necked doves came year on year to nest; at first some distance away, nesting in the golden conifers by the fruit cage; flying each morning to sit on the roof of the house and coo to each other. As we sat only feet away from them on the rear patio, we would enjoy their communication in the early morning and evening before they went to roost. After a couple of years we would still notice them on the roof of the house and on the steps leading from this area but they no longer flew to the golden conifers. Walking towards the house one morning a gentle guttural coo made me stop at the junction of the paths, just six feet away from the house. Two feet from the path, within a straggly *Weigela*, sat the dove on a platform of sparse twigs, cooing gently. My heart stood still. Wrens nested yearly on the north wall about three feet from the ground, tucked within the growth of the honeysuckle. Other wrens gathered in warming groups amongst the

271

ivy on the outbuildings and on the northeast wall of the kitchen, protected by the glossy evergreen foliage of *Pileostegia viburnoides.*

§

Although we opened the garden to the public so much of the atmosphere of it was still very private. No one but us saw the dawn light bathe the three pines or the colour of their bark lightened to pinkish-brown. Very few had experienced the slight mist that rose at this point in the garden; hanging with eerie effect to about ten feet in the air. I often wondered what Arthur and Gay had thought when they planted these specimen pines in a group of three directly in front of the house albeit at quite some distance. Did they ever envisage the statement they would make fifty years later? Did they expect to live long enough to see them grow to such elegance? I don't know the answers to these questions. What I do know is that Gay loved these trees. We used to stand together in the pine litter that gradually killed the grass beneath; chatting and encouraging the children to bounce on the softness. From spring through summer, Orchards gave joy to visitors, whatever the weather, but few saw the garden after it closed at the end of October; when deep leafy carpets of gold, red, maroon, orange and yellow covered the ground. Only close friends would walk with me in those months, kicking up leaves and taking in the aura of Orchards. It was a childhood friend, Juliet, who walked with me one autumn, ankle deep in golden hornbeam leaves, and reminded me that it was serendipity which allowed me to work in this piece of heaven.

The rising sun sent shafts of pale lemon light through the naked silver birches, reflecting from their stems and glistening on the filigree of the branchlets and twigs. *Betula youngii* - planted by me in 1979 on the west side of the front vista - an unnamed hybrid and *B. pendula* 'Tristis', planted by Arthur on the east side of the vista gave buttery-yellow autumn colour. Because of their varying habits, these birches took on a difference appearance when washed by the same rays of sun. Arthur's birches were probably fifty to sixty years old. They stood tall and majestic, their bark, capturing any luminosity so that they almost glowed and looking especially dramatic against a backdrop of dark grey sky. On clear days if viewed from the steps behind the house, against an azure blue sky, the effect was magnificent. I liked them best in winter when the light caught the minutest droplets of rain or dew on the naked twiggy stems. Because of the maturity of these trees the shadows thrown at ground level had a drama of their own.

The evening light also had a magical quality; it lifted my spirits and gave a great sense of wellbeing. The back, shoulder and neck ache, scratches and cramps of the day become worthwhile, with my daily fix of the beauty of the garden. One of the most heartening sights was from my office window. The evening light on the *Quercus robur* f. *fastigiata* was extraordinarily stunning, especially in winter. This remarkable tree, of which there are only a few specimens in England, is an upright form of the common English oak. The outline was splendid, like a giant candle flaring into the sky. The branches thrust upwards fifteen to twenty feet in length, shorter in length at the top as it tapered off. I would touch the rugged bark and lean inwards gazing aloft through the canopy. The fissured bark was covered in yellowish-green lichen. The placing of this specimen by Arthur and Gay was perfect to catch the setting sun. Even on a grey evening; the sunset quite often sent a flash across the garden which lit up the oak and the *Magnolia grandiflora* nearby with its large felty backed leaves hanging twisted; some glossy green, the reverse orange-brown like a huge patchwork quilt. On the other side of the oak, there stood, the aptly named *Gleditsia triacanthos* 'Sunburst' further adding to this radiant flash, which could be momentary; so brief that, in reaching for the camera, it had gone or changed to a less striking effect.

The Scots pine was Philip's favourite. The lower branches had been removed when autumn and winter winds had snapped them. The umbrella of dark green needles above the trunk of pinkish-red bark was a joy. On a summer's evening we would sit on the back patio as dusk darkened to night, in the ever changing light, different mysteries and atmospheres would reveal themselves in the garden. Again the tree shapes had the greatest impact, strangely darker and more austere against the navy-black sky. In late spring, and early summer we would sit, contemplating the day's work, with the *Magnolia tripetala* gently rustling overhead. By autumn its huge leaves would be fully grown and changing yellowish-green, no longer a waiting room for nutty nourishments. The birds had been busy - nesting around the garden - sometimes quite dangerously. I often wondered why most robins nested on the ground.

The tweeting of newly hatched fledglings would draw Saffron's attention; often I was too late to stop her inquisitiveness. Around us bats would swoop and dive; keeping at bay the midges and mosquitoes.

The mature trees planted as a shelter belt on the west and north sides of the plot had developed into a lovely woodland walk; with a mixture of native trees; birch, holly, ash, yew, rowan, hornbeam and several common oaks. Through the branches of one mature oak scrambled a 'Kiftsgate'-type rose which then cascaded downwards from sixty feet or more, a rippling mass of single white flowers in clusters which filled the air with sweet fragrance during the month of June. Beneath their canopies grew many interesting shrubs and small trees. *Rubus* 'Benenden' hung lax branches covered with single white flowers, like that of a wild rose. *Halesia monticola* - the Silver Bell or Snowdrop tree - flowered in late spring with or without its silky mid green leaves. *Cercis siliquastrum* - the Judus tree - was tucked behind another now mature copper beech, which Gay had grown from seed. It was hemmed in somewhat so we removed the lower branches of the copper beech. The magenta flowers growing directly from the main stems of the *Cercis* could then be glimpsed from a distance in late spring. *Buddleja alternifolia* - a deciduous shrub with silvery-green leaves and fragrant lilac flowers that garlanded the arching branches in early summer - sat just outside the canopy of the copper beech. The grass under the beech and *Cercis* was sparse; this was one area where we introduced woodchip to create paths, which meandered in between the trees and shrubs. *Davidia involucrata* - the dove or handkerchief tree - was also overrun by the sweeping branches of the copper beech. With the hedges around Arthur's old bungalow matured; the best view of the spherical white bracts, from which the tree gets its name, was from the farmer's field on the other side of the farm lane!

Standing at the northwest end of the woodland walk was *Cercidiphyllum japonicum* - the Katsura tree. With its autumn hues of yellow, orange and red set against the butter-yellow of the three large hornbeams, it was a magnificent sight. Added to this, the fallen heart-shaped leaves emitted a burnt sugar aroma when crushed beneath your feet. *Clethra alnifolia* - the Sweet Pepper bush - had a suckering habit. Candles of fragrant white bell-shaped flowers from late summer onwards were followed by good autumnal colour. A spindly specimen of *Cunninghamia lanceolata* was tucked in the top woodland nearby the back boundary. It had survived the neglect of many years - the top woodland was one of the last areas we tackled during our time at Orchards - but was left only for sentimental reasons and not for its beauty. Sheltering beneath the canopies of mixed native trees grew *Camellias, Rhododendrons*, small flowered *Azaleas, Cornus mas, Hydrangeas* and *Viburnum tinus* seedlings.

§

When I look back at how we transformed Orchards I am still full of wonder as to what inspired me the most. Was it the tranquillity? Or the beauty of the newly unfurled leaves on the trees in April and May? The *Robinia* and *Gleditsia*, generally the last to come into leaf were like wallflowers at a dance waiting to be asked, the buds so fat but not yet open. Against a cerulean sky, they looked like jewels. So much had happened by May. The garden never slept, there was something to look at; something to admire; something to make me smile. Was the inspiration instilled in me by Arthur and Gay? An idyllic thought. Was it the birds; the robin who ate from my hand, the ring-necked plovers that nested in their see-through platform so close to the path? What stirred my soul the most? Was it the fresh new foliage of the herbaceous plants; lime green, pinkish-green, gold, maroon, dark green or silver - waiting to burst into summer splendour? Was it the early blossom of the cherries, *Amelanchiers*, *Lonicera fragrans* and *Oemleria* on the bare stems of winter? Or was it the snowdrops, hellebores, and *Scilla messeniaca*; the early *Camellias*, the late *Camellias*, *Azaleas*, *Rhododendrons*, fragrant *Viburnums*, *Epimediums*, honesty, bluebells, wild orchids in the apple tree meadow; the *Claytonia* covering the corrugated roof of the old wooden shed years before flowering roofs became fashionable? I never really knew what it was. The simple truth is that I was just inspired.

Complete joy was the emotion felt when looking through the windows to the garden outside. The view through the kitchen window, across to the heather and conifer garden which gave colour throughout the year was a constant. A large straggly specimen of a pink-flowered *Erica* x *darleyensis* still bloomed well after fifty years. I remembered this from my early childhood; the crisp papery texture of the pretty pink flowers. We left it neglected, not wanting to risk losing the plant if we cut it too severely. Although the main structure of the mature trees altered little over time, save to cast more shadow; the herbaceous planting was like an ever-changing tableau. The early spring growth brought a more diverse colour spectrum to this evergreen display. The closest view of the garden was from the kitchen, where you could enjoy the raised border under the *Magnolia* tree. Fresh green leaves of hardy *Geraniums* and Welsh poppies were overshadowed by pretty blue *Scillas*, polyanthus and the marbled leaved *Arum italicum*, along with snowdrops and dwarf daffodils. This aspect altered dramatically throughout the year and by August required severe cutting back. Loved by the different finches; taking *Geranium* seeds to feed their young and in turn introducing them to the same delights when fledging. Initially we only saw bull finches but in later years, greenfinches, chaffinches and siskins joined them.

Beyond the *Magnolia* foreground was the Yew border. Planted in 1990, the yews matured to create a solid backdrop of dark green, which was in sharp contrast to the herbaceous planting in front. During the winter and early spring the bed resembled a 'white label graveyard', where I had marked the previous years' planting schemes, like an artist pencils sketches before painting. The seasonal transition was breathtaking, as nature worked her magic and made my vision a reality. The west end of the border was predominately yellow, orange and red planting; many were daisy-shaped flowers; possibly my favourites. The different shades of *Anthemis tinctoria* 'E. C. Buxton', 'Kelwayi', 'Wargrave Variety' 'Sauce Hollandaise' and of *A.* 'Grallagh Gold' linked together in graduating heights made a river of yellow from the back of the border through to the front where *Coreopsis verticillata* 'Moonbeam' and *C.v.* 'Zagreb' jostled for space with bronzed leaved *Carex comans.* A ribbon of blue-flowered English *Iris* - *Iris latifolia* threaded through the border. These blooms were followed later by generous clumps of *Iris germanica* its many bluish-violet flowers held on the sparsely branched stems - the fans of grey-green leaves evergreen in the milder winters. *Iris sibirica* - large plantings of which were in the garden during my childhood - evoked distant memories. To them I added many more, *I.s.* 'Lady Vanessa' with large wine-red standards and deeper falls and *I.s.* 'Pink Haze'; whose warm pink flowers would

281

unfurl in late May. These were two of the fourteen different cultivars I purchased. It is now, as I look through my index cards, I realise that I was probably obsessed with *Iris* as well.

A number of *Iris* said to have originated from the garden of the late Cedric Morris were given to me by a member of the Hardy Plant Society. We made a special border surrounding the old swimming pool for these. Many visitors didn't see the value of this genus in the garden claiming them to be short-lived in their flowering time but I loved them. I was fascinated by their grass or sword-like foliage, in diverse shades of green or grey-green; the formation of the buds; thrusting like spears to the sky, gradually unwrapping one petal after another until the standards and falls draped open to the sun like a newly emerged butterfly. *Chrysographes*, another Siberian *Iris*, with flat linear grey-green leaves, the stems carrying two fragrant, dark red-violet flowers in early summer with gold streaks on their falls became a difficult but firm favourite. I also grew Dutch *Iris* and particularly loved 'Bronze Queen' coloured a bluish-bronze with amber-yellow falls. Arthur grew but a few; the delicious toffee, chestnut brown shades not readily available when he made the garden. We would drool over the colours at the Kelways nursery stand at Chelsea. I added a few *Iris reticulata* to the spring garden too, planting them in pots in the cold frame and plunging them into the garden as they came into growth; removing them again once they had flowered.

As the weeks passed from spring to summer, the borders would explode in a sea of colour. On the Yew border, the acid yellow bracts of shrubby *Euphorbia nicaeensis* were softened with plantings of shorter growing *Miscanthus* species and allowed an easy blend of colour, to the pale blue-flowered hardy *Geraniums*, the lilac of *Polemonium* 'Lambrook Mauve', the pink-flowered *Geranium* 'Elizabeth Yeo' and the deep violet heads of *Allium* 'Globemaster' and *A.* 'Purple Sensation'. An erect clump of *Galega* x *hartlandii* 'Candida' also gave late summer and autumn colour; an easy plant to grow and propagate. *Stipa gigantea* competed in height through the season as it grew to its full glory of eight foot long flower stems in autumn. In front of the *Stipa* was a trouble-free *Salvia nemerosa* 'Amethyst'; its airy spikes of small pinkish-blue flowers lasted well into autumn.

283

One nursery customer had asked me for *Salvias* which 'died back tidily'. I had never considered that to be important but he had a valid point. Close observation of the many different species I grew proved that some didn't die back as tidily as others. This could be applied to many other plants, shrubs and trees. Maybe as I had so much to enjoy in the garden, I would turn my eye to something more lovely. This customer only had a small garden, so to him the entire lifecycle of his chosen plants was vital. Very little deadheading needed to be done to *S. n* 'Amethyst'; the very structure of its growth made it interesting even in the winter months.

Salvia forsskaolii, described as a tender perennial, overwintered with us as long as the flower stems had been retained. From the deeply lobed, rough basal green leaves - some of which would grow to twelve inches in length - branched stems carried white tube flowers with violet lips. I found this easy to propagate from seed. Rosemary Verey had introduced me to this genus, giving me *S. uliginosa* - the Bog Sage. Hardy, but needing moist conditions, it struggled in my over-endowed borders. I grew a great number of *Salvia* including *S. farinacea* 'Victoria' for summer bedding in front of the veranda. The vibrancy of the deep blue flowers and stems made it a 'must have'.

The centre of the Yew border would cause me concern in every July. Gaps began to appear where a plant had been cut down or where deadheading had altered the structure of the planting. Self-sown forget-me-nots and love-in-a-mist combined well with the early flowering hardy *Geraniums*. The forget-me-nots were removed and used as mulch around the apple trees, enough seeds being dispersed on the ground for next year's blueness. Meanwhile the feathery foliage of love-in-a-mist continued until the seed heads had developed, swollen with ripeness, a soft hue of green, gradually flushed with maroon until they became papery and beige in colour; the segmented tops opening to reveal jet black seeds. Accents of red were introduced at the west end of the border with *Penstemon* 'Cherry' a free-flowering red, *P.* 'Burgundy' a wine-red and *P. digitalis* 'Husker's Red' with maroon-red foliage and white flowers blushed pink. Black-red leaved *Dahlia* 'Bishop of Llandaff' gave autumn colour along with *Crocosmia* 'Walberton Red', with large red flowers and handsome pleated green leaves. The deep purple-red *Knautia macedonica*

285

was a choice plant - its long straggly stems could be woven amongst others nearby - it gave a continuous show of 'button' flower heads. An added delight was seeing them when frosted by the first snap of winter.

Bold statements punctuated the border with many different cultivars of *Kniphofia*. The robust spires of *K* 'Percy's Pride' - greenish-yellow in bud, turned canary yellow, then matured to cream. *K*. 'Bees' Sunset' with honey-coloured bottle-brush shaped flower heads and the diminutive *K*. 'Little Maid' with spires of pale yellow, tinted beige aging to ivory from pale green buds their subtle hues blended well.

The steps that lead past the *Magnolia* border on the left, up to the grass in front of the Yew border completed this view. More than twenty terracotta pots of ornamental grasses stood on these steps: originally planted for my closer observation as I learnt their structure, gave me continual pleasure. Most of them were tactile and the diversity of their flower spikelets was delightful to observe close up. These steps were awash with *Alchemilla mollis* - despised by many as weedy - a firm favourite with me; the lime green flowers merged against the aging stone steps, and were ideal for pressing for use in my flower pictures and

286

cards. On the right hand side of the top step was an *Acer dissectum atropurpureum* bought at Bodnant in 1979. This tree was of interest all year. The bare red-tinged stems, the early grey-tinged spring leaf growth, the delicate red flowers, flowing through deep purpled-red foliage to fiery maroon, in autumn. Through this lovely specimen I encouraged *Clematis* 'Kermesina' (described by the late Graham Stuart Thomas as *'warm claret-crimson'*) to snuggle against the leaves, like jewels in a crown.

§

The garden took on a new magic if viewed from above. One of the most nostalgic views was from the east facing bedroom. This was my bedroom when I was a child. It then became my children's bedroom when we returned to live at Orchards after Gay's death. When I first moved back it was from here I would gaze with mixed emotions, at the neglect and chaos of the borders, whilst absorbing the beauty of the textures, colours and patterns of the shrubs and trees. In those early days, before the transformation had begun, the southerly view from the lounge was completely obscured by an upright conifer; planted as a dwarf in Arthur and Gay's day. They had laid sandstone steps in

287

front of the sunroom doors, down to the front vista. On either side of these Gay had planted different heathers and dwarf conifers. In the early 1970s conifer gardening was a popular alternative to cottage gardening.

Unfortunately a number of the 'dwarf' conifers did not remain dwarf forever. They could be very slow growing for a number of years and then they steadily grew more quickly. We watched the growth of this conifer over a number of years as it edged itself skywards towards our bedroom windowsill and gradually past the window. For several years a pair of greenfinches chose to use the top of this conifer as a nesting place. We couldn't resist watching them. Laying in bed (we rarely slept with the curtains closed) we could see them balancing precariously on the tips of the branches, tiny pieces of nest building material in their blunt beaks; taking a fleeting look around before darting inside. With eggs laid and incubated, both parents flitted backwards and forwards feeding the youngsters. We felt sad when we made the decision to reduce the height of the tree by half. Would the finches return? They did the following spring; but this time we viewed them from the lounge window instead. With the conifer reduced in size by several feet, the view from our bedroom was now the same perspective, which Arthur and Gay would have had. However theirs would have been of a less mature garden; with the newly planted specimen trees and shrubs resembling dots in the grass. What thoughts did they have? The infancy of the garden and surrounding woodland would certainly have afforded them a different outlook to the one we had. They would have been able to see the Church of St. Leonards in Turners Hill village. As a child I could watch, through a telescope, the cricket team playing in the distance, on the field behind the Red Lion pub.

The view to the southeast of the library window had a less permanent cover of green; but the shades and textures proliferated. *Cryptomeria japonica* Elegans Group changed colour like a chameleon through the year. I liked it best in its winter coat of rich mahogany. In front of this we planted a *Laburnum* x *watereri* 'Vossii' moved from elsewhere as it was becoming overshadowed by faster growing specimens. This cultivar had longer golden-yellow racemes in spring and early summer. Nearby the *Cryptomeria*, was a huge pampas grass, moved with Arthur's help in the

1970s as it was too close; but still the gap narrowed. Against the pampas grass we planted a *Cercis canadensis* 'Forest Pansy', a truly beautiful plant that glowed maroon against the pampas. The rich colour of the conifer replacing the *Cercis* once the leaves had dropped. The red theme began in spring with a red-leaved cherry with deep pink flowers, followed by rich deep foliage of *Acer platanoides* 'Crimson King', still a small tree in comparison to its more mature neighbour *Acer griseum* which delighted us in autumn with its brilliant scarlet colour and peeling cinnamon bark. Within this tapestry were the subtle hues of the red-leaved oaks *Quercus rubra* and *Q. cerris.*

In the distance to the southwest grew some of the finest conifers in Sussex. The beauty of conifers planted with space to grow is understated. A sixty-two foot high x *Cupressocyparis leylandii* 'Naylor's Blue', dominated an area of the garden, spreading towards a large clump of *Rhododendron ponticum.* Long forgotten beneath the grass was a brick driveway - laid by Arthur - to bring building materials up the garden to build the house and to bring water drawn from the well for the animals. We discovered this when we tidied the edges of the twin long borders. The view from the library window in the failing light made me draw breath at the beauty of the garden. I remember Gay telling me that in the summer she would float on her back in the swimming pool after putting us to bed, just to gaze at the trees around her. Now I understand the tranquillity she felt. Light changed the garden all the time. When most people would be pleased with hot sun and clear blue sky; I realised that the garden was often more beautiful in the half-light of dawn or dusk.

The different shades of green never ceased to surprise either. The dark green spreading junipers tinged with gold in the spring, the limey-green of *Robinia pseudoacacia* 'Frisia', backed by the greyish brown trunks of a group of unnamed pines. This particular grouping of trees was magical. The sun would catch the trunks in the morning as it was rising and again in the evening on setting, bathing it again in soft light. The pines must have been an early planting judging from the photographs taken in the early 1940s that show them looking full and stumpy; by the time I left Orchards they had grown to such a height, cleared of the ivy set to choke and spoil the beauty of their trunks. Crows and magpies would sit on the very top; looking out over their territory. Adding my own flair to the garden's already established structure was a joy and a passion. I planted *Sorbus aria* 'Lutescens' and *Acer pseudoplatanus* 'Brilliantissimum' as companions to the *Robinia* - planted by Arthur many years earlier. Sadly the *Sorbus* snapped at ground level during the hurricane of 1987. The *Robinia* also took a battering from those violent winds and lurched forwards, its surface roots pulling up from the soil. It remained at a precarious tilt. It was too heavy to push back up. We removed a couple of branches to lighten the weight from its crown, but still it leant hazardously. We backfilled the root plate with mole hills and mulched it annually. Once the garden was open to the public we supported it with a prop. The *Acer* was a bad placement on my part - the stunning shrimp-pink spring foliage clashed with the pink flowers of *Prunus* 'Kanzan'. I had seen this *Acer* in leaf on a visit to Powys Castle in Wales one spring in the late 1970s. Several were planted together with stunning effect. The delightful shrimp-pink is quickly replaced with boring, dull yellowish-green leaves for the summer months. Mistakes were part of the learning curve and often informed future decisions. Many combinations of old and new plantings worked extremely well.

The silvery-backed willow-like leaves of deciduous *Elaeagnus angustifolia* were muted by a nearby conifer. The tiny creamy-white flowers filled the air with sweet fragrance in summer. A variegated holly towered above the layers of the juniper; rising ever upwards trying to catch up with the *Robinia* in height. It had dipped its lax branches to the ground and layered at every opportunity. We removed the lower limbs leaving the layered pieces, these were cut over with the small mower; leaving an unusual prickly ground cover.

In the early 1990s I planted *Photinia* x *fraseri* 'Red Robin' behind the root plate of the *Robinia*. This left us with two options. If it flourished and the *Robinia* remained it would look stunning, its reddish new foliage and more mature leathery, rich glossy leaves against the acid yellow of the *Robinia*. On the other hand if the *Robinia* failed, then the *Photinia* would take over. Next to the *Photinia*, I planted an unnamed eucalyptus which we coppiced every couple of years to retain the height; selling the young leafy stems to a local florist. Nearby I planted *Fagus sylvatica* 'Dawyck Purple', a purple-leaved columnar cultivar of the common beech. It would have given better colour in more sunlight but it still delighted with strong

293

purple-green foliage through spring to autumn until leaf drop.

Did my parents realise how large these *Juniperus* x *pfitzeriana* would grow; their flat layered branches reaching out, closing the vista; creating the perfect place for a grass snake to bask in the late spring sun? These textures of green were lifted with spring flowering *Rhododendron* 'Pink Pearl'. A layer removed from a neglected specimen of pale pink flowered *Magnolia* x *loebneri* 'Leonard Messel' - where long branches swept the grass in the top arboretum and rooted - established well nearby the deep pink flowers of *Lavatera* x *clementii* 'Bredon Springs'. This little border was underplanted with *Pulmonaria saccharata*, hellebore seedlings and a rash of transplanted snowdrops. *Hydrangea macrophylla* 'Nigra', a black-stemmed cultivar with dark green leaves which turn darker still in the autumn and rose-pink flowers and *Hydrangea paniculata* gave colour until the first frosts. Below this group dripped my *Betula pendula* 'Youngii' which lead down the garden to other borders hidden from view from the house.

§

What vision Gay and Arthur must have had. To stand in this field looking down a slope, wondering how to begin to make a garden. In the early days the decision may have been made easier by circumstances beyond their control. The house was finished, the war had begun, whatever their intentions, the grass in front of the house was fenced off and cows put to pasture. The sheds were filled with goats and chickens. Ducks were kept in triangular arcs and fruit and vegetables were grown in abundance. Did they plant the orchard for the war effort or was it their way of coping with the amount of land they had bought? Did they want to be self-sufficient?

One story Arthur told was of him standing with a colleague outside the house; perplexed as to where to begin. In a distant field stood a mature beech tree; he was advised to use that as his focal point. The house sat almost south facing in the plot and the main vista took a southeasterly line. Over the decades the beech tree was lost from sight and the vista narrowed with the maturity of the trees; the foliage melding together like an artist's impression. Once the garden was open to the public; we shortened this vista further. Many visitors began their guided tour from the bottom of the garden.

In order to 'hide' the garden from immediate view to visitors we developed an area around an existing weeping cherry. 'Cheal's Weeping Cherry' now called *Prunus* 'Kiku-shidare-zakura' stood nearby *Rhododendron* 'Cynthia', both dominated by the height of other mature conifers and specimen oaks. In twenty years this *Prunus* barely reaches a height or spread of eight feet. It gave spring and autumn interest with large, double deep pink flowers in profusion on pendulous branches. The new foliage is bronze maturing to mid green during the summer and a bronze-orange in autumn. The initial border we created around this cherry was an irregular shape and took in 'Cynthia' and the daffodils that flowered nearby. After the daffodil leaves had died back and been cut in June we mulched well over that area and killed the remaining grass. When grass persistently reappeared through the mulch we killed that too; turned the soil and mulched the new border. We added more shrubs to this border; *Choisya ternata* 'Sundance' for its bright gold leaves and fragrant white flowers, *Oemleria cerasiformis* for the almond fragrance in late winter, striking *Rhododendron* 'President Roosevelt' with green and yellow variegated foliage appeared even more dramatic against the reddish pink-edged flowers of late spring and early summer. *Hydrangea macrophylla* 'Möwe' flowered over a long period - a deeper red-purple in the acidic conditions of this part of the garden.

For winter colour we chose *Cornus alba* 'Elegantissima' and *C. a.* 'Spaethii', the former had the same red winter shoots as *Cornus alba*, with white flowers in flat cymes in late spring and summer, followed by white fruit often tinged blue; its grey-green foliage margined irregularly white. The latter, while similar to *Cornus alba* has green leaves broadly edged yellow. We also added *Cornus sericea* 'Flaviramea' for its vigorous growth and bright yellow-green winter shoots. *Salix purpurea* 'Nancy Saunders', an elegant form of the purple Osier with slender blue-grey leaves carried on maroon stems, made an excellent plant companion in the spring with its soft silver pussies glistening in the spring sunshine.

I enjoyed the placement of *Potentilla fruitcosa* x 'Basil Fox', a handsome shrub, named by me after the late Basil Fox who I met in the 1970s whilst on a trip to Wales with Arthur, after Gay's death. He was Curator of Botany Garden, University of Wales, Aberystwyth. During this visit we were shown around the nursery established in the Botany Garden. Basil Fox gave me cuttings of a pale peach-flowered *Potentilla fruitcosa*, with permission to propagate it for use in the garden whilst he was alive. After his death it was sold in the nursery as *Potentilla* x 'Basil Fox' named in his memory. It was planted in several locations around the garden; the peach colour of the flower more intense in shady spots.

This border, once established, succeeded in 'hiding' the view of the house and front garden from arriving visitors. It was underplanted with *Geranium monacense* x var. *anglicum* and *G. phaeum* seedlings, *G. macrorrhizum* 'Ingwersen's Variety' and *aquilegia* seedlings. They were complemented by *Papaver somniferum* seedlings which grew much like a weed but they were welcome for their pretty presence was enchanting; from the glaucous crinkly leaves to the tight buds which disgorge tissue paper petals in both single and double forms; fattening to bluish-grey seedpods for autumn interest. *Luzula sylvatica* and *Acorus graminea* 'Ogon', *Lamium maculatum* 'Beacon Silver', a low growing ground cover with silver leaves narrowly margined green and clear pink flowers; tall striking *Iris sibirica, Epimediums,* primrose, snowdrops and *Muscari* gave year round pleasure. During the winter of 1999-2000 the rain barely ceased; the area above this border became sodden, water rose down the path which edged the lower orchard and flooded around the golden conifer. The tree died and need to be removed; the Cheal's Weeping Cherry also died. This border then became known as the Oso berry border after the *Oemleria.*

§

Encouraged by Anne Boscawen, who, with her husband the Hon Henry Edward Boscawen, owned High Beeches in nearby Handcross; I made contact with TROBI (The Tree Register of the British Isles). Originally a friend and colleague of Arthur and Gay; Anne stayed in close contact with us whilst the garden was open to the public. In October 1999, Dr Owen Johnson, Assistant Registrar of TROBI came to see the garden. He measured all the significant trees. These were important not necessarily for their rarity but for the maturity of some species, no longer in cultivation. He listed thirty-one that he considered to be of 'national importance'.

We accumulated a number of friends and volunteers during our time at Orchards. Long standing friends and family came to help with teas on open days or in the nursery. Over the years, several ladies volunteered their time to help in the garden - some gave assistance for only a few weeks, some for a few years - their support was a valuable contribution to the running of the garden. It was well understood that any 'payment' would be in kind: happy to take back home a little piece of Orchards in the form of a cutting from a treasured plant; vegetables, apples or eggs from the hens. Many were equally generous with plant material from their own gardens.

Julie Hollobone arrived as a nursery visitor and asked for paid employment. She needed practical gardening experience to go with an RHS qualification she was working towards. At that time there wasn't a budget for paid 'staff' but she was welcome to gain as much practical experience as she wanted. Looking to further her career in horticulture, we agreed that Julie could hold the first gardening workshops at Orchards; on different garden techniques; pruning, climbers and simple propagation, amongst other subjects. The garden was used as her studio. Philip refurbished an area next to the tea room, installing benches for her propagation classes. Enterprise Travel arranged a few garden visits to Orchards in the spring of 2000. Out of the blue and with very little notice they asked if a talk could be put together about Orchards for the evening before their initial visit. Julie and I worked on the presentation together. Julie gave this first talk using Arthur's antiquated slide projector. Many other talks were given to horticultural societies and garden groups in the locality over the next couple of years. We would travel together sharing our story and the experience of Orchards; I would take plants and cards to sell after the talk.

We would garden together, often sharing ideas and thoughts on ways of doing things. One day we were tying up the herbaceous plants on the Yew border that had escaped from their earlier staking. So luxuriant was the summer growth of the planting that we could hardly get into the border. There was certainly no room for a trug to hold string, scissors and stakes. I stuffed the string down the front of my vest top; tucking the nail scissors under the straps. Julie shook her head with despair.

'You're so haphazard in all that you do.'

'Great title for a book.' I replied.

Once qualified, she was able to procure employment at West Dean College, in Sussex. She went on to write a book on propagation techniques and to write a monthly column for a gardening magazine. As I write she may have moved on to even greater accomplishments.

It was through one of the workshops at Orchards that I met Victoria Jane Heasman. She was like a breath of fresh air. She bounded along the path, so excited with the results from her first attempt at compost making. She was the same age as my daughters; already married with three children. She was vibrant, hardworking, and enthusiastic and became a very good friend. On a whim and without consultation with Philip I rang her and asked her to consider working for me. She squealed with delight. Anyone who could be that excited about compost making was the right person to work with me. At our next meeting I explained about our very limited budget. We discussed the number of hours she would work each week for this amount. When we next met she said she would accept the sum offered but would work as many hours as she could manage over and above the agreed amount because she liked us, thought what we were trying to achieve was wonderful and most importantly, that she knew she would learn an enormous amount from me. Vikki was wonderful and flexible in any and every job she was asked to do. As my health deteriorated we would still garden together; I would fill the wheelbarrows and she would run them up the garden to the bonfire or compost bins, and back for me to fill again. We worked in all weathers - many times in inclement conditions - hoping that Philip wouldn't return early and send us indoors. When working outside was absolutely impossible she would do housework for me instead. I know that our relationship caused offence to some of the other volunteers. However they were already experienced; and to my mind, it would have been an insult to offer them the same amount I had offered Vikki.

Well meaning friends and volunteers who sought to impart their will and comment on the way we gardened were not welcome. None of my friends or acquaintances had quite the same situation, neither were they of the same opinion about what Orchards represented; seven acres of parkland to some peoples' thinking and a mere patch to those who had a garden ten acres or more. All circumstances were relevant and although I did with some self-importance, wonder why

303

anyone with a small patch should leave it untidy, when I knew that with my expertise it would take no more than an hour to straighten; I resented the same comments about my garden. No one else I knew gardened on the same scale, within a mature garden, with the limited amount of help we had. And of course, few people realised just how much 'running' the garden cost in monetary terms.

One such acquaintance that came as a volunteer mused and commented often with disparagement, until sometimes she left me downhearted and dispirited. *'Less is more'* was a favourite theme, thrown at me like some kind of insult about my way of planting in abundance. Garden design was not one of her qualifications, so I was unsure as to how she formed this opinion or arrived at this conclusion. Abundantly planted is how I liked my garden to look. My daughter Sorcha often told me that I was like an artist in the way I created borders of colour. Whilst I enjoyed the creativity and artistry of my border plantings; I didn't like them to appear contrived in our woodland setting. Oh I don't disagree that I lost a few treasures on the way, because I did things unconventionally and learnt the hard way that I needed to pot and nourish some, standing them on the steps near the house where they could be more closely admired and sometimes it made me rethink plantings. The same volunteer was also offended with the bright pinkish-purple of my clove pinks against the sunny yellow of *Origanum vulgare* 'Aureum'. I saw these same 'clashes' in meadows all the time and marvelled at nature's ingenuity.

I was quite happy with a huge clump of *Kniphofia* 'Atlanta', which could be viewed from the front terrace. Its thick channelled grass-like leaves and tall upright coral-red flower spike which faded yellow, standing proud with *Ilex* 'Golden King' - or was it Golden Queen'? - as a backdrop. To the fore curved stems of *Crocosmia* x *crocosmiiflora* 'Solfatare', with apricot-yellow flowers and bronze foliage were set against white-flowered *Libertia formosa*, and the different yellow tones of *Rudbeckia* 'Goldsturm' and *Geum* 'Lady Stratheden'. Nearby this I had planted *Centaurea dealbata* 'Steenbergii', its intense dark carmine cornflowers, with greyish-green leaves set contrasted against *Iris sibirica* and looked stunning.

For several years the *Kniphofia* had finished its flowering before the *Centaurea* came into flower, but with the onset of milder winters the two seemed to catch up; flowering at the same time. The blue of the *Iris* was acceptable to me, the coral-red and pink not so much. I chose not to acknowledge the clash, casting my eyes instead towards the blue *Iris* and pink cornflower and associated plantings or towards the statuesque holly with *Kniphofia* to the fore. It is true that I did not have time to spend evaluating the plantings in great depth, possibly the truth is I quite liked the occasional lack of harmony; it gave a more natural feel to the planting. However after much discussion, and with my defences lowered, I removed the *Kniphofia*. Some were sold, others replanted on the other side of the border away from the pink *Centaurea*. With delight the *Centaurea* took off in all directions but I missed the early season colour of *Kniphofia* 'Atlanta' against the holly, so the *Centaurea* was removed. *Kniphofia* 'Atlanta' had won and was swiftly replanted in front of the holly. The entire length of the border was widened to take an even more interesting and varied range of planting.

Another old school friend - a keen flower arranger - always said with a tut-tut *'You should leave room for the butterflies!'* when she saw my crowded vases. She didn't appreciate the posies of garden flowers I gathered by hand and arranged whilst walking around the garden. Nor did she like the way I summarily trimmed the stems to length and placed them unceremoniously into a vase; usually a crystal one belonging to Gay. This was my way - a similar jumble to meadow - and long before hand-ties became fashionable. This friend went to flower arrangement classes and in her opinion rigid rules had to be observed. Mounds of foliage were needed 'to green up' I believe the floristry term is, within which were poked at uniform distances, the correct height of whatever flower, usually carnations or chrysanthemum in the late 1970s and 1980s. For me it was another example of qualification taking precedence over experience or creativity. I greeted this phrase with the same lack of deference as the 'less is more' theme. The butterflies in my garden never behaved like that. Very rarely did they go in; they balanced precariously on the sweetest part of the blossoms, usually in the sunniest position. The only insects I have seen go inside flowers are bees, wasps, ants and earwigs. From this you will gather (and be correct to note) that I had a wild, unkempt attitude to my borders; borne out of necessity. Or was that just my excuse?

307

I was once asked by a gentleman garden visitor whether there was any particular reason why I might have planted *Acanthus spinosus* so close to the lawn and so many of them at the back of the long border; 'That's where nature put them,' I replied.

'Could you not remove them?' he enquired. 'Or move them further into the back of the border with the others?'

'Have you ever tried to dig them out?' I countered. 'They have a taproot that takes a direct route to Australia!' To be honest I liked the way they looked, without any effort they broke the straight rigid line of the long border, the foliage of the ones closest to the lawn were cut several times during the season, therefore fresh young leaves were always present.

Annie Bridges had been buying my plants from the local farm shop before I opened my nursery. She became a reliable friend and was one volunteer who expected nothing in return. She made cakes for our NGS and other charity open days, as did some of the other volunteers; refusing any payment for the ingredients needed. She would also come and serve teas for the private groups we had, help in the nursery or shift compost. Sometimes she only had half an hour to spare but in that time she worked hard. Often Vikki and Anne worked together with me.

When I didn't have volunteer help or Vikki working with me, the birds were my friends for the company and entertainment they gave and for their dutiful pest control. Many people perceive birds to be the biggest nuisance in the garden and some of them can be. We wondered at the increase in the numbers of the birds and whether they saw us as friends and the instigators of this delightful sanctuary. Our two cats Smith and Jones respected the birds and, to our knowledge, never caught them, but did catch mice and baby rabbits. Philip fed the birds throughout the winter. It took a while for some of the birds to work out how to use the new ceramic feeding which hung from the *Magnolia* outside the kitchen window. The lesser spotted woodpecker took the longest time to devise a method of wrapping himself around it in order to peck. The woodpecker returned the following spring. We watched for several minutes as he flew to the *Viburnum opulus* 'Roseum' down the under-levels to the black pussy willow, down again to *Rhododendron* 'Elizabeth' back into the *Magnolia tripetala* where the nut holder hung from a low branch. He took some time to shuffle

309

forward moving with a series of little jumps; pressed as close to the branch as possible, nearer and nearer to the nut holder - eventually he landed, clinging precariously pecking out the last morsel of nuts within. Saffron (realising that this length of observation must indicate something interesting) whined with anticipation. I scooped Saffron up in my arms. Sorcha was watching the behaviour of the woodpecker too; she grabbed the camera, dropped to her knees and shuffled out of the kitchen door. This excited Saffron even more; she leapt from my arms and licked Sorcha enthusiastically. With all this commotion the woodpecker flew away.

Much time could be wasted watching the different birds from the smallest, goldcrest and wren, which tended to forage in the undergrowth from dropped crumbs of nuts, to the marsh tits, black caps, blue tits on upwards in size to the spotted woodpecker. With delight we would watch blue tits loading their beaks with moss from the sandstone wall, pulling and collecting in their tiny beaks and flying up to the box on the north wall. Wherever the birds decide to nest, we showed them respect. One year a wren nested under my outside potting bench. I moved a few feet away to work and she continued with her maternal duties.

Blackcaps made their nests in the cracks of the sandstone wall. Frequently spellbound by the sense of tranquillity and peace at Orchards, in particular during spring, the sound of the birds was a welcome part of my day.

My memories of the birds in the garden at Orchards were not only visual or idealistic. I recall the way a pair of ring-necked doves cooed to each other; how the robins squabbled and blackbirds fought, squawking fierce 'words' to each other, chasing through the garden like missiles; but they all sang for the sake of singing. I used to talk to the robins - residents of the garden who have a reputation for being quarrelsome - but we found them no more so than other birds. They would cock their heads to one side listening and then reply. The blackbirds did the same.

§

In 1995, Philip became my husband as well my best friend. He worked full time elsewhere; returning late afternoon to start work in the garden if the light or weather permitted. By high summer he would have to drag me indoors to relax before bedtime. There was always some job to be finished; it was impossible to fit all that needed to be done into twenty four hours. We had worked at the same company in 1989 for a few months before the recession took its toll and we were both made redundant. Philip found employment easily. I eventually found a part-time job as a receptionist/secretary at a local tree surgeon company. This employment although brief, was extremely useful. I learnt even more about trees and shrubs, their canopies and how to maintain or reduce them. It also gave me the opportunity to consult on a couple of gardens and draw up planting plans for them.

The owner, Bill Matthews was an old family friend; he too gave a lot of welcome advice; but I also made two valuable new friends. Bill McWhirter, who should have retired years before I went to work there, but held in such high esteem by several longstanding clients that they would only allow him to consult on their gardens. After his retirement he moved to Scotland. For a few years he stayed with us in springtime, pruned the apple trees, visited nearby friends and gave us all the advice we needed. When he was no longer able to travel, my vivid descriptions of various tree problems were detailed in my letters to him. Full and helpful replies came back supporting our project. It was Bill who, in a diplomatic way, persuaded us that the squirrel damaged copper beech should be removed. We had left the tree for two years after the damage had been done but Bill advised us that (given all the hard work that Philip and I had put into the garden) a failing, copper beech of such proportions was out of place. Showing extraordinary kindness, he took himself a ladder and a handsaw and began pruning the lower branches from the trunk, leaving only the main body of the tree for Philip to deal with.

The other firm friend I made at the same company was Chris Coomber, a tree surgeon and more importantly a climber. His help was possibly the most precious, certainly the most practical. He could be persuaded to do almost any job for us; often calling in on his way back from a days' work. Many a day, Philip arrived home (hoping for an early evening) to find us tackling trees or finishing off bonfires. Chris taught me the art of bonfire making. Arthur would spend hours in unsuccessful attempts to get a good roaring fire, starting with a tiny pile and gradually adding to it. Chris was much bolder and more expert; he started with a huge mound of both paper and dry wood, once alight he laid the wood across it, not like a wigwam as was traditionally thought to be effective.

This ensures heat in the heart of the fire, later the outer debris is drawn in and across the centre but laid flat not leant. This method saved time and effort; and if you were strong enough, large branches could be slapped on the top. Sometimes the height of the flames scared me but Chris always knew the measure of the flames and the time it would take for them to diminish.

Chris Coomber, Penelope & Saffron

His payment; Sunday lunch, the occasional supper during the week, eggs from our hens, vegetables and apples from the garden, jars of homemade jam and chutney and - most importantly - a mutual friendship that has stood the test of time.

The garden at Orchards became as much a part of life for Chris as it was for us. He didn't wait for a call requesting help with a job; he arrived on a weekly basis if not more often. Sometimes just for a cup of tea and a piece of cake but always eager to know if there was some way he could help. Once he came after a busy wind had blown through the top arboretum pulling apart the group of *Thuja occidentalis* 'Rheingold' which had been moved by Arthur in the late 1970s into a horseshoe shape. Perpendicular branches, too mature to tie back in - leaned out at odd angles. The shape of these lovely trees was lost but I felt that to remove so many of them in one area would be a mistake. Philip and Chris thought differently. The majority won the day.

By the end of a busy afternoon they had been all been felled, the brush burnt and the stems logged into neat piles. The guys were right. Light flooded the opened area to the existing trees and shrubs. The pretty grey-green, white and pink margined foliage of A*cer palmatum* 'Butterfly' brightened; an untidy mound of weeping silver pear, *Pyrus salicifolia* 'Pendula' became even more disorderly; a distant vista of *Fraxinus* *angustifolia* 'Raywood' now dominated, clothed in its claret-red autumn colour.

Around a nearby group of white-barked *Betula utilis* var *jacquemontii* we made a grass garden for the taller grasses growing in the garden. The glossy foliage of *Prunus laurocerasus* 'Otto Luyken' spread wider, carrying its fragrant white candle-flower racemes in spring and frequently again in autumn. Glimpses of the *Camellia Grove* could now be seen through the ornamental grasses and the white birch stems. The white bell-like flowers of *Styrax japonicus* tucked behind the grove dripped above the dark green *Camellia* foliage in early and mid summer. To the side of this group an *Acer palmatum* seedling - grown by Arthur from a seed in the late 1950s - twisted and curved its aged branches; the foliage glowing rich deep red in autumn giving dramatic contrast to the buttery-yellow autumn tint of the *Stryax*.

Despite the fairly temperate Sussex climate, occasional winds whipped through the garden often causing immense damage at the most inconvenient of times. A mature specimen of *Liriodendron tulipifera* often drew admiration. The large interesting tulip-shaped leaves, tinted bright yellow and limey-green in

316

September added to the autumnal colours, although the flowers were rarely seen. The lax branches were allowed to sweep the grass; a solitary cup-shaped flower bloomed at eyelevel; an exquisite shade of pale green banded pale orange at the base of each of the petals. Every garden visitor was told of this delight. The night before a charity garden opening a complete limb - at least one third of its entirety - was torn from the tree. It resembled an enormous 'heel' cutting. The flower was on the ground amongst the debris. With no time to clear the spoil before opening; visitors were directed to it, to see the ongoing challenges of running and maintaining a woodland garden. Chris called in the following day; tidied the ravaged tree and dealt with the branch that had fallen. Other twiggy bits had snapped off and embedded themselves like javelins several feet into the ground.

One of the major tree removal jobs that Chris undertook was to fell a tall conifer which had shed its top onto one of the polythene tunnel in my working nursery. Luckily, only one metal span was damaged, foreshortening the tunnel by a few feet once repaired. We debated the importance of this conifer for some time; already growing on the edge of an overcrowded

317

shelter belt where competition for water and nutrients was keen. Even without the six feet of top growth it had deposited in the nursery, the remaining tree was still seventy to eighty feet tall. Could it be trusted to keep itself intact? The limb it had shed showed no sign of disease but the decision was made. It took Chris three days to fell the conifer piecemeal. The upward growing branches had to be roped and carefully lowered one at a time until a naked trunk was all that was left. With absolute precision he brought this down in one section along a strip of grass. The only damage was a channel along the turf, where the weight of the trunk had thudded to the ground. The brush took a further week to burn. The wood was logged and stacked and left to season, providing fuel for many years to come. The stump remained; soon encircled with foxgloves, primrose and other spring plants.

§

Chris also gave Philip assistance with the construction of the cabin during the winter of 1999/2000: after another guy Vic Friend had levelled a piece of ground near the selling nursery. Vic had been called upon on several occasions to undertake major ground works. He was paid for his labour but his prices were generally kind. As a child, the area near the stream which ran through the lower part of the garden had been known as the bog garden. We were advised not to go through there, not only because Arthur had planted it up with many choice bog plants but also because when it became very wet it could be a little dangerous. Many a time I lost my Wellington boot in the sodden ground; straggling home to Gay who would be very cross that I had disobeyed her and that my socks were laden with mud. In the late 1970s Arthur asked the local farmer to scrape the area into a pond shape. The soil in this part of the garden was heavy clay. Around this Arthur planted a variety of suitable specimens - most of which did not survive.

In 1995 we asked Vic to enlarge the pond. Philip supervised the operation, advising where he wanted the soil hollowed out and moved to and at the same time introducing other narrow channels to take the water from the farm lane into the pond. Over these channels Philip constructed wooden bridges from redundant telegraph poles. On raised decking built in the middle of the pond Philip made a little timber house. We were quickly rewarded by a pair of Mallard ducks setting up home, safe from the wily fox. The Pond garden (as it came to be called) was developed further. The *Gunnera manicata* planted by Arthur had matured into a stunning specimen; the prominently veined, kidney-shaped lobed, toothed leaves gave drama beneath the Swamp cypress - *Taxodium distichum* - now a ragged mature specimen. Bamboos planted on the opposite side of the stream screened the little woodland that ended the garden's southerly boundary. A simple chestnut paling fence edged the lane and the lower drive; initially to keep stray dogs from frightening the wildlife. We added numerous plants to this area; *Hostas, Hemerocallis, Lobelia, Rodgersia, Iris, Lythrum, Lysimachia, Lysichiton americanus, Euphorbia and Mimulus.* Sadly with so much else to do at Orchards this area was never opened to the public and because it received less attention than other more important parts of the garden *Petasites japonicus* very quickly ran riot.

The top section of the bottom orchard which Arthur replanted in 1975 was too crowded. He had planted the new trees in rows of four instead of three as in the other orchards. I am not sure why this had been done; possibly because they may have been on a more dwarf rootstock. Whatever the reason they did not grow well, the maturing oak trees on the west side of the area stole more light from midday onwards. Philip grubbed out the first few rows except for one specimen 'Ashmead's Kernel'. This sweet, slightly acidic russet apple was introduced in 1720 in Gloucester. The skin is one of the prettiest of its type; a bright green-yellow flushed with orange and a wash of cinnamon. The next few rows were thinned so that only two trees grew alongside each other. The older trees planted in rows of three were all 'Lord Lambournes'. In many ways it was a shame to grub out this deliciously sweet apple. We took a lot of criticism from the Sunday walkers along the farm lane; but we were used to this. 'Have you ever stopped to take the windfalls offered in autumn?' I would ask. The reply was always a negative coupled with a good reason for not doing so. 'Do you prune your own trees?' would be another of my counter responses. This would also be met in the negative: inevitably they paid someone to do the job for them. A great deal of satisfaction was felt with these replies; we wished them good day and continued with our work.

In his day Arthur would begin pruning the numerous apple trees at the beginning of November and gently make his way a tree or two a day, leaving twiggy debris around each like a fallen skirt until usually on Christmas morning whilst waiting for lunch, he would finish the last tree in the bottom orchard. Boxing Day quite often had us gathered in the orchards grasping large armfuls of prunings to take to nearby bonfires.

We fenced the cleared orchard area near the driveway but left it untouched for a couple more years. As my nursery business picked up, the concrete drive was insufficient for more than a few cars. In preparation plants were removed from the long border that edged the old orchard. An enormous lorry came one morning; the turning circle for it to reverse into the driveway too restrictive - he skidded and massed up the soil even further as he forced himself into the square of grass we had set aside for cars to park. A small mountain of chalk was dumped; followed by two or three more loads. Vic appeared with his machine - a pull-you-push-you contraption moved the chalk mounds around, diminishing them in size until a thick layer of chalk lay on the grass. Once rolled flat, more lorries came with a top layer of scalpings; this too was rolled flat and pounded down. By the time they had finished we had a car park with space for at least a dozen cars if they all parked with respect for one another. We took care to ensure that the Ashmead Kernel's roots were protected by a narrow ring of bricks. Around the fence line we pushed in cuttings from willow and *Cornus* which rooted readily along with native seedlings found in the garden and woodland.

Vic was called upon once again to dig out a driveway in the top orchard above the selling nursery. It would be a good car park for nursery visitors; and we required soil to infill the old swimming pool. One row of trees had succumbed to the worst foe - honey fungus - the remaining trees bore very little fruit. They were retained but given a severe canopy reduction. The leaky old swimming pool was possibly the last eyesore for a garden that was growing in reputation. I was glad to see it go. The summer had to be very warm for me to want to swim; and the girls were growing up and too busy with other things to be that bothered.

On a hot August weekend Vic came with his digger and dumper which Philip drove backwards and forwards across the middle of the garden. Tons of soil was dumped into the pool from the newly created area for the nursery car park. But more was needed. In the area near the Cheal's border where the trees had been flooded and consequently died, a ditch was born. This area had remained moist for the last few years. At one end, Vic (with Philip's guidance), dug a bowl shape which narrowed to a curved ditch; water leeched from the higher ground into the bowl immediately and trickled down the garden towards the old shed. It was almost as if they had uncovered an ancient spring. The neighbouring woodland had a similar structure of ditches which we would play in when we were children (land belonging to someone else; as if our own eight acres weren't enough). It was only in the winter that these ditches became filled with water. Maybe when Arthur and Gay first arrived at Orchards there had been similar ditches that they had infilled?

A stack of new railway sleepers originally destined for my cabin borders were utilised as new bridges across the ditch. Two bridges were laid; each three sleepers wide. By the end of a very productive weekend, the pool had been filled in to above the brim and a new ditch garden had been created! After that our thoughts turned to the development of the Pool Garden; to take the late Cedric Morris's *Iris* collection.

The white border made in 1991 had never really worked well. Set against the east wall of the house it was never a true white border as the existing wall plants

324

all had varying hues of pink! But how could you remove a plant that had survived this world for as long - if not longer than you - just because it didn't quite fit in with your plans? Adherence to the white colour scheme was therefore not strictly observed. I had read that white flowers did better out of the glare of the midday sun, so an east facing location seemed to be a perfect location. The border was successful from spring until midsummer, except that the white campanulas flowered blue, the white foxgloves were pink; and the native red poppy punctuated the front of the border - poppies were a favourite so had to stay - and then the border failed. The plants were moved to the crescent prepared in the swimming pool area; this became known as the pink and white border with no consideration given for the midday sun. Here there was sun throughout the day. The narrow lawn that followed the curve of the semi-circular and edged three sides of the old pool was removed, the sloping sides levelled. Philip capped the edges of the old pool with paving and replaced the existing slabs which ran along a narrow border on the fourth side. On three sides a narrow railway sleeper border was constructed with sleeper steps leading to the cartwheel bench. The *Irises* were planted in these narrow borders, where the rhizomes could bake in the sun.

The recently placed soil within the old pool was left to settle - it was my intention in the following years to make a rose garden on this large rectangle. In its first year I sprinkled wild flower seeds; the result was not as successful as I would have wished, possibly because of the lack of water or maybe the birds found them a tasty meal. The following year I seeded the area with *Cosmos*. How I love *Cosmos*: their feathery foliage, the open structure of the petals, the delicate colours of white and pink shades to the stronger deep red. They enjoyed their sunny location and could be seen from the office window flowering above the six foot yew hedge. They grew taller here than in any other position in the garden.

Before we moved the plants from the white border the crescent-shaped garden behind the old pool had been stripped of everything except one unnamed *Philadelphus*, a white *Buddleja*, a large specimen of an unnamed poplar with white leaves and grey reverse. The latter was reduced to a stump and very quickly we were rewarded with new shoots. Every couple of years we coppiced it - the leaves became larger, the colour

326

more intense. Through the summer carmine-red *Clematis* 'Ville de Lyon' and *C. viticella* 'Purpurea Plena Elegans' a smaller double violet-purple flowered variety, threaded their way up and through the stems. An established but unruly *Escallonia* with deep pink buds opening to pale pink was ruthlessly pruned to reduce its size and make it more manageable. The ancient *Lonicera syringantha* that we moved from the end of the scrubby long border - so straggly and neglected that barely a dozen sweetly scented flowers bloomed against the stems - was replanted here. We gave it a severe haircut and kept our fingers crossed. Weeks later, the umbrella shape we had pruned it into was covered with tiny green swellings heralding new leaf growth. We planted *Choisya ternata* 'Sundance' rescued from a friend's skip and *Viburnum plicatum* f. *tomentosum* 'Mariesii'. To balance the other end of the curve a white-flowered, dome-shaped *Hebe* was introduced. Ground cover and interplanting included *Paeonia* 'Bowl of Beauty', *Geranium* x *riversleaianum* 'Mavis Simpson', *G.* x *r* 'Russell Prichard' and *Leucanthemum* x *superbum* 'Phyllis Smith', one of the most delightful of the shasta daisies whose shaggy white petals appeared as if they'd been cut with a pair of scissors. *Erigeron* 'Foersters Liebling', *E* 'Schneewittchen, tall white *Alliums*, snowdrops, pink hyacinths, white and pink lily flowered tulips all added to the mix. The copper beech hedge was the perfect backdrop for the plants. Around three sides of the old pool we laid gravel and edged the crescent with Victorian style edging. The pink and white border became known as the Pool Garden.

Naming the borders became essential. We could no longer say to each other we were gardening 'up the back' or 'down the front'. We needed to be more specific. It was also very therapeutic; especially when Vikki was working with me. Depending on the time in hand, you could feel you had achieved something by setting yourself a task to deal with one of the named borders. Besides the sense of purpose this gave us (and the practicality of being able to locate ourselves or the plants within the acreage), the devising of these different areas - each with their own character - created an ambiance of intimacy, in what was a very large expanse of land.

The border leading to the greenhouses became known as the Chestnut Terrace (because of the chestnut stakes wired at the top to hold back the soil). The narrow border that edged the path beneath the Chestnut Terrace (under which lay the water pipe) was planted with *Geranium endressii* and *Nepeta racemosa*; within a couple of years the *Geranium* had completely smothered the *Nepeta*. This edging was cut a couple of times a year with the hedge trimmers; growing back fresh light green foliage within days; the bright pink flowers blooming on ever shortened stems. The border above was planted with low growing herbaceous plants, the raised area above that, with *Ceanothus thyrsiflorus* var. *repens, fuchsias*, sea lavender, *Galtonia candicans*, *Camassia leichtlinii* and the subsp. *suksdorfii* 'Blauwe Donau', *Scutellaria altissima, Iris unguicularis;* many *Geranium sanguinium* cultivars, *Diascias*, as well as orange and peach *Alstroemeria* rescued from Arthur's greenhouse after he died. This planting was backed by the *Lonicera* hedge of the Herb Garden.

The long back border ran from the east to west ending at the new kitchen garden. The east end of this border was backed by the shrubs that Gay and Arthur had planted. A second specimen of *Kolkwitzia amabilis* had been placed at the furthest end, as well as a small tree of *Buddleja globosa* a favourite species with tight balls made up of numerous orange flowers, *Viburnum plicatum* f. *tomentosum* 'Mariesii', *Cotinus coggygria* Rubrifolius Group, *Lonicera nitida* 'Baggesen's Gold' and a *Rhus typhina* nearby the *Kolkwitzia amabilis* that dripped over the sandstone wall, leaving spent blossoms like pink confetti on the patio. The *Rhus* was loved and hated in equal measure. I cherished its brilliant autumn shades of yellow, orange and red and for its candles of maroon seeds; but loathed its invasive suckering habit and the effort it took to trace back a sucker to be removed. But on a positive note, when the original plant had been tipped over by a strong wind or looked sad for some other reasons: (which had happened on more than one occasion) a sucker would be left to develop nearby, and then the older specimen removed. A very easy means of replenishment. On the west side of the steps, *Salix gracilistyla* 'Melanostachys' with beautiful red-anthered black catkins in late winter and early spring. (This had been given to me by a friend as thanks for my help with her garden); *Magnolia tripetala*, *Viburnum opulus* 'Roseum' and *Rhododendron* 'Elizabeth' now thrived.

As we linked the specimen trees into borders, these too were named after the more mature occupant. Under the naked stems of *Gleditsia triacanthos* 'Sunburst', a

330

colony of *Eranthis hyemalis* as bright as a buttercup (to which family it belongs), shone vivid yellow above a ruff of bright green leaves, an early reminder of the gold leaves to come. New borders were made with an introduced specimen. A wedding gift from Rosemary Verey remained a few years in its pot before we found a place to introduce it. It became the key feature in the *Cornus controversa* 'Variegata' border - aptly named the Wedding Cake Tree after the layered 'tiers' of its branches. This border was parallel to the east end of the long back border. Cut in the shape of a kidney - the roots of the nearby cherry dictated this outline - the *Cornus* and *Spiraea* var. *japonica* 'Goldflame' were the only constants, in an eclectic mix of herbaceous plants and bulbs that coloured this little garden through spring, summer and autumn.

The *Prunus* 'Kanzan' border was developed at the end of one of the twin long borders. I have pictures in the early 1980s of a tangled mass of overgrown shrubbery with the cherry branches sweeping so low that the visiting deer could feed from it easily. There were many treasures found on this part of the border. The cherry had been a specimen nearby the twin borders but the thicket of *Neillia thibetica* had suckered

331

into the grass and joined the cherry. An unnamed evergreen *Berberis* had created a grove; its lax branches touching the soil and layering new growth. A smaller cherry was completely obscured from view by this on the one side and a small tree of *Osmanthus* x *burkwoodii*. In the middle of this chaos of growth two moss-type roses scrambled. One was identified as *Rosa* 'William Lobb'; the other carried a smaller flower similar in colour and sweet fragrance. *R.* 'William Lobb' was removed and placed along the fence that backed the selling nursery. The other remained in its position with a strong wooden structure erected by Philip against which it was partially tied to four feet and then given the freedom to scramble at will into the nearby cherry. On the other side of this cherry, I planted *Rosa* 'Paul Transon' a large flowered fully double salmon with coppery overtones and a creamy-yellow base on each petal. It rambled rapidly along the branches and through the canopy, enjoying both the shade and the sun. Its fragrance of fresh apples filled the air drawing attention to its beauty. Both the *Neillia* and the *Berberis* were severely pruned back and the layered stems dug out and removed. The grass beneath the *Neillia's* onslaught had died over the years. We took advantage of this - and laid a curved woodchip path - Chris was having woodchip dropped for us on a regular basis. We would spread it directly onto the soil, and tamp it down with the wheels of the tractor and trailer. This was extremely helpful as wood chippings were used for many of the pathways. When the well trodden grass paths became slippery and dangerous during wet periods; the chippings made an inexpensive and safe option for walking totally in keeping with the environment.

Linking the specimen trees and shrubs, by creating new borders, actually made the garden look smaller, more intimate and compact. At the end of the day - and what a long day - seven and a half acres, is seven and a half acres; and despite the increased opportunity to introduce more plants in the newly formed areas, it did actually make our life easier as the years progressed. The grassy areas beneath the trees were killed, chippings or mushroom compost spread as thickly as time and money would allow and after a few months the borders were underplanted with a diverse range of plants and small shrubs. The garden never ceased to delight us. Barely a week went by without a new show of flowers or leaves or both. Huge clumps of daffodil bulbs planted by Gay and Arthur in the late thirties and early forties were transplanted to these areas. Several hundred more were moved, from the newly formed grass paths into the borders until we could face no more of them. One twelve inch clump of daffodils afforded over two hundred bulbs and daughter bulbs; which flowered even more prolifically once divided. With this done the grass areas became smaller and the borders became larger. This worked very well. A neater more unified garden evolved, though with a woodland naturalistic feel.

Philip cut the grass at least once a week during the season. All the grass took seven hours if he did the job. He knew the best way around the garden for time and economy of petrol. When Stuart, a longstanding friend of ours, took over the grass cutting he was well advised by Philip of the route to take. Stuart was a great help to us after my surgery in 2002; not only did he work in the garden (allowing Philip to continue working full time), he also took good care of me. He ran my bath, cooked my breakfast and lunch. He brought logs in for the fire and made me comfortable with tea; leaving an hour before Philip was due home. Given strict orders from my consultant to do nothing it made my inability to do any kind of work - heavy or otherwise - just a little more tolerable. Thanks to Stuart, that was the only winter when every single leaf in the borders, paths and grass was raked and composted, and I didn't have the heart to tell him we left them on the borders!

A good gardener cares and tends to their plants as if they are small children. A lack of knowledge can make some tasks very daunting. Traumatic is how one customer described pruning to me. Even when armed with a good book, with excellent diagrams showing the exact cut to make, they feared cutting into a stick with no signs of life. When training Vikki; her trepidation was obvious. I instructed her to return later to observe a recently pruned plant. Pruning *Sambucus nigra* 'Guincho Purple' had been overlooked in the previous year. Even when we went to tackle it, I could see the swollen purple buds waiting to burst. Vikki wanted to cut higher to one already flourishing. She was convinced that all my cuts were too low. My explanations about it growing six to ten feet from a 'stool' were falling on deaf ears. Returning to the elder later in the summer she marvelled at its growth and fully understood why she should follow my advice.

The keener, more committed gardener I became, the more important the weather was to me. Not one to be bothered with the exact hours of sunshine in the area or the amount of rainfall we had each day or week. Come to that I wasn't too concerned about the temperature in the greenhouse or degrees of frost on the ground. The weather was, after all, out of our control. However it did dictate what we would be able to do the next day. Gentle rain was most appreciated. Seeping rain that hangs in the air; permeating gently through the soil. The plants and trees almost held themselves upright as you would in a warm shower; soaking up the bountiful wetness. The leaves and stems seemed to embrace the drops like a sacred pool. As a 'daily' gardener what the weather chose to do was as important for me as it was for people who had 'real' jobs; those who sat in an office for most of the day, with only the weekend to enjoy the garden. Working in the garden and nursery brought its limitations in monetary pleasures but I would have rather have been out in the garden any day. Come to that even now I would rather be spending money in a specialist nursery than a clothes shop!

During our time at Orchards our limited appraisal of the weather for the next few days would determine if the help we had with the garden was summoned or not and even then the weather didn't behave as had been forecast. Stuart spent many desperate hours on the tractor until saturation point was reached; he was fed and sent home early. Vikki's flexibility and willingness allowed her to undertake many different tasks; working its way down in importance to housework.

I seldom watered the garden or the lawns; the grass invariably recovered after a dry spell. I had long ceased referring to the lawns as 'lawns'. My grassy areas were full of delightful daisies and blue speedwell and moss. Occasionally moss was raked out but not very diligently. I rarely spiked the lawns either nor brushed silver sand over. Once you have seen the nesting birds pulling the required amount of sphagnum moss from the lawn for their nests, we were never to keen to take away their supply.

The size of the garden brought its own limitations in its care and maintenance but the plants in the pots were another matter. The sale plants were the most important; in dire circumstances the plants were moved onto grow-bag trays so that the watering would be of real use. The pots on the steps were given saucers for the same reason. After a lot of rain, more time was spent removing them. It was a joke amongst family and friends that the plants either drowned or died of drought but with so much to do, it was hard to be on top of everything. The gardeners who visited understood the vagaries of the weather. Philip frequently phoned from London to ask how much rain we had had. None was often my reply, as he travelled down the M25 seeing rain in the distance, it would be wet on the roads towards home but the farm lane to Orchards would be dry as a prairie. Once, as a small child Arthur and Gay woke me in the night and sat me on the dining table so I could look out of the window and watch fascinated and a little scared at the storm outside; huge flashes illuminated eerie blue light across the garden, you could see a narrow band of rain make its way down the centre of the front vista. Storm watching with Philip came to be a pleasure. We would perch in the veranda (not on the dining table) sharing our thoughts on the spectacle unfolding before us.

I had a fairly naïve - or maybe modest - attitude to opening our garden. Even though the garden was always 'work in progress', we wanted to share our 'patch of heaven' with anyone who wanted to come and see it. And they came in their hundreds over the years.

So many were glad to be able to see where Arthur had written his books and drawn his inspiration. Many more were captivated with the effort that Philip and I were putting in and the mark we were making together on the plot. Of course this allowed some criticism from some visitors but they were the ones who had no idea of the challenge we had undertaken. One came in stiletto heels, pushing a buggy, looking for the playground! Some complained that our lawns had no crisp neat edges, some that the ground was undulating. I could only reply 'Tell the moles to go away!' As the years went by the challenge grew stronger. With hailstones which hurled themselves one afternoon in July laying so thickly that it looked like snow; whole borders could be destroyed in a few minutes. The winds would flatten even the most carefully staked borders and snap huge branches from the trees. The *Liriodendron* was not the only victim. One morning we woke on a day of opening for the NGS to find that two trees had fallen over in the top arboretum. An apology was all we could give. The visitors I enjoyed the most were the ones that looked past all of this and could just take pleasure in the garden for what it was - a truly magical place. Fortunately those visitors were in abundance.

Many came back throughout the seasons to see the changes - not only in the borders, trees and shrubs but also to buy plants that became available throughout the year.

We were becoming more aware of other people's expectations of us. On one of our open days a lady stopped me in the garden and asked if I would like to be included in the 'Good Gardens Guide'. Several people had recommended the garden and she had visited unannounced to view it for herself. We were included for the first time in 1999 and remained in each annual edition until we gave up the garden. In fact, despite that the house was on the market and could possibly have been sold before the book was published, they retained the 2005 entry; in the hope that the subsequent owners would want to continue to open to the public.

§

It is fairly sound advice to plant what grows locally and to know your own soil conditions but if Orchards were ever to be transformed into a housing estate, the houses at the very top of the garden would be surrounded with peaty soil from years of deciduous leaf mould. Whereas their neighbours, further down the plot, unless into building sandstone walls - would curse. A few inches of good soil, where the old vegetable garden was, gave way to a stratum of solid sandstone. It has been said that it was on this stratum that the building of the house was originally planned. If this is so the early excavations by hand would have revealed thick yellow clay and sandstone. The old photographs of the completed house in 1938 show a dwelling looking marooned and out of place; set on the top of the slope. The nearby farm, house and barn are clearly visible. With the mature garden of today the house was positioned perfectly. The area Arthur and Gay dug for the house must have had its own problems, because in the immediate vicinity of the house was solid yellow clay. When we dug out the back patio it revealed a depth of only three to four inches of good top soil. Further down the slope with mature planting, no great depth had been dug. The shrubs that had been planted required only a spade depth, maybe a little more. Any houses built at the bottom of the plot would revel in water or bog gardening. The clay here is solid, grey and white.

We didn't want a housing estate to be built but would, as my health deteriorated and more paid help was becoming essential, have liked to build at least one house on the land to sell. The site of the original wooden shed; completely obscured from the house could have been easily integrated into the garden. However with a 'blanket ban' on property being built in our area; permission would have been refused. We sought the help of a local and county councillor who undertook direct communication the various departments on our behalf; we were reliably informed that the response would be negative.

One day Philip and I were walking along Worth Way the site of the old railway line which Beeching closed in the 1960s - where as a child I had heard the 6.45am train toot his whistle going over the bridge, as Arthur opened the door with my cup of tea before he left for work. Reflecting on the future during this gentle stroll - a few weeks after my surgery - I conceded to a deadline of our sixtieth birthday (we share the same day and year) to be our time to consider giving the garden up. We talked about where we might live once we made that decision. We couldn't reach a conclusion. A knee operation followed three months after the previous surgery. I had a busy year ahead of me - one week after my operation, with the aid of crutches, I escorted my first group of visitors around the garden. The nursery stock was less; propagation being impossible either before or after my operations. Vikki and I had worked as hard as we could but the two years leading up to surgery and other health issues had put us so far behind. With my inability to sustain the amount of work the garden required, the slow realisation that our departure would be sooner rather than later dawned. There was no way that we could sit back and watch the garden fall into neglect once again.

I was locked in a memory - trapped in a dream. I was in love; I think I always had been. I was in love with my garden. The backache it caused was forgiven - the long days and aching knees were almost relished for all the beauty, peace and tranquillity it afforded me. Some days exuded even more joy - visitors who gave admiration; customers who filled the homemade trugs with my 'babies'. When I could look with pride at a potful of loveliness that I had created, nurtured, cleaned and which was then carried with equal pride by the buyer who had coveted it. The books were full of orders, rarely were the customers disappointed. I could easily divide or root another baby for them. There was no stopping me in the beginning - I rushed around like an ever changing wind from one job to another. But I started to look back and realised how difficult it had become to sustain that energy.

'Your garden,' enthused one elderly gentleman at the end of a garden visit, 'is like a comfortable old overcoat.' These words were like a warm embrace. It was not just the more advanced in age that enjoyed and understood the garden and the way we gardened it; but the most sympathy and appreciation came from them. They understood only too well the slowing down process, the reduced strength that age brings on, notwithstanding the health issues I'd carried with me throughout my adult life. The borders at Orchards often brought back memories of their childhood gardens; usually on a much smaller scale, when large gardens with affluent owners were rarely seen unless you worked in them. That elderly gentleman (and others like him) loved that we grew the Shasta daisy, black-eyed Susan and golden rod which their parents had grown when they were children. I totally agreed - gardens are all about memories.

The decision to move to Italy was made in a flash. The realisation that the time had come to leave this beautiful place was like the beginning of a mourning process. We would travel we decided, find that dream place - very difficult when you already live in a small patch of heaven. I had childhood memories of Italy; but I was too young to remember or appreciate much. Sorcha was engaged to a delightful Milanese man. She was already travelling the world; it became obvious that her life would not be in Sussex anymore; she was to live in Italy when she married the following year.

A country girl at heart, the big city should have been intimidating but I found it exhilarating. Our first trip to Milan in 2004 was uplifting - the architecture, the people - so friendly and accepting - the glass-roofed Galleria - where designer shops, restaurants and a MacDonalds were all clad with black signs with gold lettering. The Galleria leads out to the Piazza del Duomo where the famous cathedral of Milan, shone with a luminosity I had never seen, but had imaged in fairytales. The piazza was busy with pigeons and people walking or standing in groups taking panoramic pictures; the wide steps in front of the duomo were littered with people sitting, talking, working on their computers or taking in the sun. Intricate wrought ironwork, frescoed buildings, huge wooden doors, delightful shady courtyards, glorious balconies; dripping with ivy and other lush greenery, rooftop gardens. Verdant parks with well spaced specimen trees; full of children, lovers laying in the sunshine, ladies of all ages sitting on benches in the shade of the huge *Magnolia* trees gossiping; men standing in groups near little kiosks drinking coffee with grappa and smoking cigarettes, dogs walking their owners along the paths. The peacefulness of the parks broken, with the hooting of cars and scream of mopeds.

Philip saw a change in me and I knew I could finally let go. My impetus for the garden's creation evolved after the death of my father in January 1993. The regime of clearance we embarked on following his death, gave us a difficult challenge. Orchards was opened for others to take pleasure in and many charities - both large and small - had benefited from the garden for fundraising. Other groups came to picnic and sketch.

Our fifteen years there had further enhanced the visionary planting of trees and shrubs. The garden had given joy to countless people who knew Arthur through his horticultural writing; both in his articles and his books. Many people had lived nearby for decades never realising that the inspiration for so many of his books lay on their doorstep. We had met elderly men

346

and woman who had helped in the garden in the 1930s as youngsters either planting trees or helping with the animals. I had made many new friends of all ages; and become reacquainted with old friends from my teenage years and old workmates too. It was the end of an era. New adventures were on the horizon, new challenges and new opportunities - a certain kind of madness is how I described it to Philip - but as one of my new friends said 'fifty-five is the new thirty-five'.

It was several months before we put the house on the market. I struggled in my head with other thoughts, other innovations which might have allowed us to remain. My first talk 'The Hellyers at Orchards' had been well received. A second one 'Shady Ladies' was being prepared; but giving talks would never earn enough money to continue the garden's upkeep. I grieved daily for the decision I had made. It was hard to image being anywhere but at Orchards.

I was sitting in the cabin preparing my accounts at Arthur's old work desk. I listened for the cars which came slowly along the farm lane; or the click of the gate or the ting of the bell which hung from one of the gate posts under which was a sign 'Please ring bell before entering the nursery'. Occasionally a passing

347

walker would amble in and take me by surprise as I'd not heard the gate, nor the bell. Ten years of business and dealing with the public in my own space had taught me a lot about the human race and I preferred (save for a small number of special people) my dog and my chickens!

I had a great deal to do; stock to sort and sell on, people to advise about the closure of the nursery and garden, accounts to close. I also knew that on this occasion we wouldn't change our minds. We would stick to the plan. It was taking time to come to terms with the decision; a period for adjustment. I lived with a perpetual sickening heaviness in my stomach brought on with fear and anxiety. Every day Philip and I asked each other if we were sure that we were making the correct choice - in between we sorted more of the debris of life. The accumulation of junk from earlier generations made this a mammoth task. I found myself rescuing Gay's old books from her childhood, relegated to the sheds after her death. These I cleaned of the white mould which patterned the outer covers and stood them in the sun to dry; the musty smell of age and dampness never quite left the inner pages but they are back on my bookshelves and have helped me tell part of her story. I felt enormous sadness at the prospect of leaving the garden - but the timing was right.

Gay would have understood, thanked me and helped me to make and standby the decision without any recriminations. She would have applauded the dedication and vision with which we had undertaken to continue their work. While out in the garden I spoke with her often and felt her presence on numerous occasions. I took her flowers from the garden to her place of internment under the old oak tree to commemorate her birthday, the anniversary of her death, their wedding anniversary and Christmas. Over the years we had naturalised hundreds of snowdrops and *Scilla* underneath the canopy.

But this particular day in the cabin, I looked up and she was standing on the veranda looking in on me sitting at Arthur's desk and smiling. Her brown gently wavy hair held back by a simple ribbon. She had on the same white overall she had worn when milking the goats. She was forty years old, not the grey-haired mother I remember who died aged sixty-nine. The image remained with me for several moments; so sure was I that it was a visitor that I looked down as I scraped back my chair on the purple carpet tiles; easing myself out of the chair I turned to the door. The figure had gone. Opening the door briskly I stepped out and looked to the left and then to the right. There was no one in the nursery. Still certain of a visitor, I hurried in a circle around the bushes and behind and to the sides of my cabin. No one was there. On my return, a robin hopped along the veranda, it stopped and watched me with its little head cocked to one side. I knew that Gay had been and sanctioned our decision with the same love and support she had always given in life.

Gay - late 1940s, early 1950s

I saw you

I saw you for a moment, a glimpse of your face
smiling. Your green eyes danced amusement,
your smile flashed the flat teeth you died with.

I saw you for a moment, chestnut waves gently
bouncing. Brown ribbon tied back wayward hair.
You smiled.

I saw you for a moment, white overall,
from your youth. Your days with goats
and rabbits.

I saw you for a moment, you're forty not
sixty-nine. You're in your youth
not gone to a better place. I saw you

I look down and scrape my chair from Arthur's desk
And you're gone. Was it you? I know it was
but you disappeared.

A solitary robin cocked her head,
watching me with beady eye inches from my feet.
No fear. I saw you for a moment
You were smiling. Now I can leave too.

© **Penelope S Hellyer**

AUTHOR BIOGRAPHY

Penelope was born in Sussex where she lived for 57 years before she moved to Northern Italy. She now lives with her husband Philip on the shores of Lake Como.

Her days are filled with writing - both prose and poetry, painting, pressed flower work, sewing, knitting and photography.

Penelope is currently working on an e-book version of The Haphazard Gardener with colour photographs, a novel, a poetry book and stories for children.

She has had articles published in The Hardy Plant Journal.

One of her poems is included in 'My Home' - Stratford Literary Competition Winners 2011.

www.penelopehellyer.blogspot.com

www.facebook.com/TheHaphazardGardener

www.thehaphazardgardener.com

Lightning Source UK Ltd.
Milton Keynes UK
UKHW042005090719
345865UK00001B/21/P

9 781781 764138